"Lady, I've Seen Enough!"

"Lady, I've Seen Enough!"

Jane Elizabeth Frist

To Rosa, my good friend, Love, Jane Frist

iUniverse, Inc.

New York Lincoln Shanghai

"Lady, I've Seen Enough!"

iUniverse books may be ordered through booksellers or by contacting:

iUniverse
2021 Pine Lake Road, Suite 100
Lincoln, NE 68512
www.iuniverse.com
1-800-Authors (1-800-288-4677)

ISBN-13: 978-0-595-41368-3 (pbk)
ISBN-13: 978-0-595-85717-3 (ebk)
ISBN-10: 0-595-41368-4 (pbk)
ISBN-10: 0-595-85717-5 (ebk)

Printed in the United States of America

This book about Grit, Grace and God is dedicated to the memory of my wonderful parents: my father, Dr. John Chester (Chet) Frist and my mother, **Lois Elizabeth** (Betty) Frist Myer.

Chet and Betty's grown children: Tommy, Charlotte, John and Jane.

My thanks to Diane Claybrook, Gigi Graham, Lynn Holman, Mary Kells and Mary Beth Thomas for their editorial suggestions. I also want to thank Gigi Graham for the use of family photos that have been included in the book.

"We have joy with our troubles, because we know that these troubles produce patience. And patience produces character, and character produces hope."

—*Romans 5:3–4 (NEV)*

Contents

Mama

o o o o o o o o o o o o o o o o o o o o o o o o o o o o o o o o

"A wife of noble character who can find? She is worth far more than rubies…charm is deceptive and beauty is fleeting but a woman who fears the Lord is to be praised."

—Proverbs 31:10, 30

One morning when my Mama and I were to eat breakfast at the Montreat cafeteria, she approached me with a piece of paper and a pen. "Here is something for you to sign immediately!" She had most likely been awake all night thinking about this. Because I had a college degree in English and was always jotting down poetry and stories and giving detailed descriptions of people and situations in conversation, she had a nagging suspicion that I might someday put something down on paper about her. She worried that it might be negative, as her brothers had given her fits as a child and called her all sorts of names, as brothers often do. Before going down the line breakfast in the cafeteria she shoved the paper and pen toward me as we sat at the table. "Here, honey, read this and sign here!" I looked with curiosity to the words on the paper that said, "I promise that I will not write about Mama or I will likely be left out of the will." This didn't frighten me at all as I knew that she didn't have much money and she had already given her four children most of her collection of antiques as well as her log cabins and some land. I do not know if I signed, but I probably didn't sign the contract because even in those days, I was intent on writing something about her someday. Probably I changed the subject. Eating became the most interesting subject for both of us. However, it doesn't matter even if I signed that paper because any contract between us became null and void when she decided to leave her money to Christian organizations.

What money she had came from her hard work, building houses or saving the $5.00 she had been given as her very own spending money each time that Daddy was paid by a couple to marry them who weren't in his congregation. Mama would have probably had a lot more money in the end if she had included halls and kitchens in the houses she designed and built.

Mama was a lively and lovely brunette who had flashing, sparkling brown eyes. She had the kind of long slim legs and full lips coveted by today's movie and TV stars. They often get their results from a treatment of Botox and from plastic surgery. Her results came from God. Perhaps she did not see herself as being the unique and wonderful person that she was. One of her descriptions in her first book, *No Wings in the Manse*, shows the following thoughts that she had about herself when she was going through the awkward teenage years. She writes, "I was made very conscious of the fact that I was an architectural ruin. I was fat and hairpin curves aren't popular in a crowded car." (Her description here is of the trips that the family took from Florida to Virginia wedged in between her five brothers and one sister.) She goes on to say, "...so I had to sit and take insults like, 'How about movin' over, Scrooge, and dividin' up a little space?' or 'Shift, butterball!'"

My Mama was the kind of person who lives on in the memories of those who knew and loved her. The memory of her causes one to smile. There were few times in her life when she did not produce some kind of reaction from those around her. I have always thought that incidents from her life needed to be told in a book. From the time I was a small child until she died, she always had a big influence on my life. I have wanted to say, "Thank you" to her by putting down her personality on paper.

Mama could tell stories that enthralled her audiences and she loved to entertain the visitors who came calling from the church congregation and from the neighborhood. As a child I would lie on the stair landing or behind the sofa and listen to her talk. I was very shy and listened intently as she enthralled the company with her stories and illustrations. She knew most of the stories in the Bible as well as most of the important Bible verses. She tried to pass them on to her children hoping that they would stay in their minds and that they would get into Heaven as a result. She felt that it was her responsibility to get us into Heaven. Even today, as Senior Citizens her children can almost quote as many verses as she knew. Her legacy to us of Bible verses is far more important than any material inheritance that we received from her.

My beautiful, fun and spiritual Mama.

Everyone said that she had a flair for dressing although she spent very little on her clothes. Some of the wealthiest women in the churches bestowed their second-hand designer clothes on her. She also had a flair for buying clothing that had been lowered 50% or more at sales. She made her large picture hats like her mother before her. They were made with decorations of colorful ribbons wound around the crown and cotton or silk flowers of all types stuck inside the ribbons. In Montreat, her best friend was a lovely lady named Ruth who she visited quite often. One day she arrived at Ruth's home in a silk dress, a small fox fur draped over her shoulders, colorful matching patent leather shoes and cat shaped sunglasses. Ruth teased her about being so dressed up in a little town where most people wore shorts, slacks and tennis shoes.

Mama's answer to Ruth was, "You never know when Montreat will become fashion conscious!"

Mama Meets Ruth

o o o o o o o o o o o o o o o o o o o o o o o o o o o o o o o o o

"Use hospitality one to another without grudging."

—*I Peter 4:9*

Mama often entertained her friend Ruth's five children by diving off the diving board at their rustic, stone-lined, mountainside pool where the water was ice cold. She would dive into the water in her silk dress, stockings, high heels and earrings as well. All the children loved the scene. She made a big splash for the onlookers! She also had a great ability to entertain them by making gorilla or monkey faces, which often embarrassed her own impressionable children but delighted the other children.

My Mama and Ruth had become friends not long after she first came to Montreat in the late 40s or early 50s. My little brother, Tommy, first introduced them. In Montreat there is a Club Program for children of all ages from nursery to college age that gives children joy. It also gives a break to the parents. They play baseball, play tennis, swim, hike and canoe. Tommy would leave home early in the morning in order to walk to the clubs. On the way, he would stop at different homes for breakfast.

Ruth's home was on his direct route down the mountain from our home, and being a friendly little six-year-old boy, he made friends with the children at Ruth's house and soon he was invited in for breakfast. Ruth was friendly to everyone and must have noticed him out in the yard talking to her children. He loved her big dog, Belshazzer, a St. Bernard from Switzerland. He enjoyed the breakfast so much that soon he was visiting her on many mornings. One day Ruth asked him, "Tommy, you are welcome to come to breakfast anytime that you want, but I was just wondering why you never eat breakfast at home." He answered her in his slow Southern drawl, "That's because I don't like dog food and Mama always gives us dog food for breakfast." "My goodness," stated Ruth, "I'd love to meet your Mama sometime. Do you think that she would like to come down here one afternoon for tea?" "Sure," he said, "she loves to go out for cokes and tea." Ruth obtained Mama's telephone number and invited her down the next afternoon. She was more than a little bit curious to meet this culinary specialist who served her children dog food for breakfast.

The very next afternoon, Mama arrived at Ruth's home. She and Ruth found that they had a lot of interests in common. They were both devoted students of the Bible, had preachers for husbands and loved antiques. Each one had a passel of children who kept them very busy. Each one was brown-haired and vivacious. After becoming comfortable with each other, Ruth broached the subject of Tommy and the dog food.

"I met Tommy some weeks ago and he has been having breakfast with us on his way to clubs. He is a delightful little boy and we love having him in our home. However, I have a personal question to ask you. Do you really serve dog food to the children for breakfast?" Mama appeared quite puzzled for a moment, but then a big smile appeared on her face and she replied, "Mercy, what in the world is he talking about? The only thing I can think of is that I often open a large can of corned beef hash, cook it in a frying pan and add catsup. I am sure he must think that is dog food since I also open a large can of dog food for Smokey, the dog, which is somewhat the same consistency as the corned beef hash." The friendship was possibly cemented between the two ladies as they both had grand senses of humor.

Ruth

Mama as a Witness

o o o o o o o o o o o o o o o o o o o o o o o o o o o o o o o o

"Let brotherly love continue. Do not forget to entertain strangers, for by so doing, some have unwittingly entertained angels."

—*Hebrews 13:1, 2 (NKJV)*

Mama could play the piano by ear, and listeners were enthralled with her joyous rendition of hymns and popular songs. She was an asset to any church, Sunday school or social gathering. Whenever she played for a congregation sitting in pews, one would notice that they would be bouncing in their seats in tune to her rinky-dink, jazzy way of tickling the keys of the piano. The overall effect was a happy one. She was also recognized as one of the best Sunday school teachers in every town where my father had a ministry. No one was bothered by her holding a wiggly baby in her lap while teaching. Her words about the Bible and its characters were fascinating. She knew stories and illustrations that few people had heard before.

If she wasn't teaching or playing the piano, she was witnessing to truck drivers at Hardees or Denny's who happened to drive up for an early breakfast. Because she arose at 4:00 AM on most mornings (a similar trait that several of her children have), she would go to a restaurant that was opened 24 hours a day. No one in the restaurant would be a stranger to her. She would smile at the person in the next booth, and whether she knew him or not, she would pat his or her hand and engage them in conversation. She would show a deep concern about their lives and ask lots of questions. Automatically, with a pat on your back or hand, and having someone look deep into your eyes and call you "Honey", one would be hooked into listening to her and into opening up about one's whole life. One felt he had known her all his life and could tell her anything. She was quick to give advice about how to solve one's problems. Most of her psychology came from the book of Proverbs in the Bible and her different counselees always seemed grateful for the help. Many times she returned for breakfast and might see the same person again and continue in the conversation from where they left off.

Some of my children's best memories are of going on the early morning excursions with her to the Montreat cafeteria or going to Denny's or Hardees for coffee and grits. They absolutely hated it when she woke them up as early as 5:00 AM, but once they were sitting with her at the restaurant and ordering food, they were hooked. She told them the fascinating stories from the Bible that she wanted to be sure they didn't miss in case their parents weren't telling them.

My friend, Gigi, reminded me recently of how Mama also drove to various friends' homes at about breakfast time, after she had been up and reading her Bible for some hours, and called, "Yoo-hoo! I'm here for breakfast." With good friends she would sometimes leave 50 cents by her plate on leaving. She never wanted to be obligated. After all, she was not a cook and could rarely have them back to her house unless it was for an afternoon of coke floats. She was an expert at making those coke floats as well as making gelatin. Cooking dinners was a huge impossibility for her to do. One of her children inherited this problem. Her talent was in entertaining, educating, decorating, painting, writing, playing the piano and cooking. A person is not expected to be perfect in all things.

After Daddy died at the very young age of fifty-three, Mama restlessly moved around the country, living in different places, designing and building houses where she was the contractor. She wrote books and served as a missionary in Mexico. Well, she wasn't an official missionary but she wanted to be. She wanted to do something good for the Lord. She just didn't know a word of Spanish. However, she packed her bags and went to Taxco, Mexico and lived for a year there, volunteering to play the organ in a small church. That is about all she told us concerning that year out of the country. Both my brother Tommy and I have been to that church in recent years out of interest in Mama's life. Mama's will left money for Christian causes and so some of this money was given to this little church many years after her time there. She would have liked that.

There are so many stories about Mama, but one of my favorites is this. When she returned home from signing books at her first autograph party after writing her first book, No Wings in the Manse, she climbed into her big antique four-poster bed where she wrote her books. The bed was always littered with small pieces of paper on which were her notes, pencils and razor blades that she used to sharpen those pencils. Daddy had to look carefully before climbing in bed beside her. When Daddy came home from the church that evening and saw her propped up in the bed writing her second book, he asked, "Betty, I guess you were pretty excited about the autograph party for you today?"

"Not really," she stated. "Why do you think that?"

"Well, Honey," he said, "then why did you go to bed with your hat on?"

Mama at her book signing party with the hat that she wore to bed.

Mama in the Nursing Home

o o o o o o o o o o o o o o o o o o o o o o o o o o o o o o o o o o o o

"Love never fails."

—I Corinthians 13:8

During the last months of Mama's life she was confined to a wheelchair and a nursing home. There was one time that she needed to travel from one state to another. It was decided that my daughter, Jane Alden, who was a flight attendant, would get a special seat for Mama in first class and help her in and out of the wheelchair. After the plane took off and Mama was settled in the big comfortable seat, Jane Alden kept trying to make the trip more pleasant for her grandmother by rubbing her arms and back. After a short while, Mama told her granddaughter to stop. Jane Alden felt that Mama was just being nice to her and kept rubbing Mama's back. Suddenly Mama let out a shrieking cry saying, "Quit it!" Half of the people on the plane looked up and stared in Mama's direction with alarm on their faces. Thank goodness it was in the days before the terrorist threats or Jane Alden might have been tackled to the floor.

In the last week of Mama's life, when she seemed to be in a coma, lying on her back with her eyes closed and silent for hours, two of her granddaughters stood on each side of her bed, holding her hands and rubbing her arms. Each one, Janie and Jane Alden, would say to her, "Grandmom, I love you so much!" They stood there for quite a while, looking down tearfully at her and half sobbing, "I love you!" Suddenly Mama seemed to come out of her deep coma and looked up from one to the other granddaughter and questioned, "Which one of you loves me the most?"

Tour of Homes

Mama's log cabins were unique in every way. The first ones she found were discovered in the hollows and back roads of North Carolina. Most cabins were tumbling down and the roofs were fallen in. Mama recognized their charm even though she may not have realized that the logs were cut from ancient chestnut trees, which were no longer in existence. I imagine that her friend Ruth introduced her to these cabins. Together they loved to scour the countryside, looking for antiques and log cabins. They found quite a few log cabins in the area of Lake Lure. At this time, I understand that the cabins were selling for as little as $25 if one would just haul them away for the owners. Mama and Ruth had numerous cabins pulled down and the logs numbered as to where they should be replaced when they were rebuilt. The cabins were usually rather small, either 12 by 12 or 12 by 18. Mama bought five, and each one made a bedroom in one of her log cabins.

Mama's log cabin.

When Ruth had her logs removed and re-constructed into a new cabin, she made certain that the building had good insulation because she planned to use it as a year round home. Mama, on the other hand, just wanted a summer cabin, so the builder was asked, as a cost-saving measure not to add much insulation. Later in life, I bought Mama's old log cabin. To this day, I visit Florida in the winter for warmth because Mama's old home, as cute as it is, does not hold heat.

When Mama lived in this cabin, it was decorated in a beautiful and unique way, as were all her homes. One day a member of the committee for the Summer Club's Annual Tour of Homes approached Mama and asked her if she would allow her home to be on the tour. She was delighted to say yes. The money from the tour would be given to young people who needed scholarships to attend the local college.

My family and I happened to be in town for our summer vacation during this particular tour. Mama was already concerned about our family keeping the guest part of her log cabin perfect for the tour. She had been insistent on our removing anything that looked modern: toasters, radios, and electric frying pans. We were to hide the two burner stove in the 4 by 4 kitchen behind an antique flip-top table. The cabin had to look like it must have looked in the 1790's. We were willing to accommodate her desires. We pushed the modern appliances under the bed and made the cabin spic and span for the tour.

Mama climbs up to the attic of her log cabin.

However, nothing was to go smoothly. Suddenly the whole family came down with the flu. The next morning, a day before the tour, all five of us in my immediate family were too ill to get out of bed. Mama came to the cabin door and asked if there was anything she could do to help. I replied gratefully, "Thanks for offering to help, Mama. What I desperately need is for you to change the baby's diapers. I feel faint every time I stand up!" With a wave of dismissal and a partial shutting of the door, she answered, "Honey, I just meant I would fix you a peanut butter sandwich or something like that." She hurriedly closed the door and headed to her kitchen for the peanut butter sandwiches. When she returned, she reminded us again of the tour on the following day. "But, Mama," I said, "We are too sick to get up and clear out of the cabin." She answered, "Don't worry.

Just pull the quilts up over your heads and we will walk through fast." Later she thought better of it and just showed the tour group the main cabin. I am sure that we were a big disappointment to her because of the flu and its consequences. She had wanted to show off that cabin. It really was cute.

One evening after Mama left from her visit to our guest quarters, my six foot four inch tall husband pulled the down mattress off the Cannonball bed that was approximately five feet, five inches long and put the mattress on the floor. He could finally stretch out and not feel the authentic ropes pressing against his back and the authentic footboards pressing his knees toward his head. He was never as impressed by primitive antiques as Mama and I were. He said, "Staying here in this cabin with the door locked is like being locked in a museum overnight and the guard has gone home with the keys!" I was reminded that when I was a child we were so accustomed to Mama's telling us not to touch or sit on anything, that my sister Charlotte at three years old announced that there was no place to sit in the house but on the john.

Mama with one of her picture hats.

Daddy

o o o o o o o o o o o o o o o o o o o o o o o o o o o o o o o o

"...and he who wins souls is wise."

—Proverbs 11:30

Daddy was a tease! Throughout his life I have always felt that, if someone teased me, they loved me. I felt Daddy's love deeply. Other people who knew him felt his deep concern and his understanding. He didn't try to change people but rather liked them the way they were. His disappointment in a person was far more difficult to bear than any spanking. He didn't spank you; he just loved you into doing right!

Since Daddy liked to tease his friends, they liked to tease him in return. I can recall several incidents that took place over the years. One Sunday after coming home from church where Daddy was the preacher, we had all settled down on our back screened porch for Sunday lunch. We liked to eat our sandwiches and gaze over the golf course that was behind our home. We lived on the 14th hole and I sometimes went out there to sunbathe until I heard the distant voices and shouts of the golfers. I always felt they were trespassing on my very own sunbathing area.

Daddy

On this Sunday, while eating, we all heard the loud jingle of a bell, coming from the area of the 14th hole. After the golfers had moved on toward the 15th hole, all of us in the family except Mama trooped out to the golf course and were surprised to find a regular red and white stop sign on a post that contained a silver metal bucket and a bell. At the top of the bucket was a small sign and a pen and paper where names were added. The sign said, "Today is Sunday. Anyone from Dr. Frist's church who missed church today, stop, leave your offering in the bucket and ring the bell so the pastor can pick up it up later."

Daddy enjoyed his life as a minister for he loved people and loved serving them. He loved his work so much that he hated to leave and go on vacations. Mama would take all four children and go to the little village of Montreat for the summer, and Daddy would stay at home preaching, counseling and playing golf. He almost had to be forced to leave town and join the family. When he did leave, he came to Montreat, following the family, but he would spend his days in the library working on future sermons. During this particular July, Mama urged

Daddy to come to Montreat for his two-week vacation. During this time Daddy was involved in a large downtown church. His friend David who was also a minister as well as a golfing buddy, preached at a smaller church in the suburbs. But it was a time when some downtown members were moving out of the city to the suburbs. He teased Daddy and said he would take some of his congregation when Daddy was out of town on vacation. This would make Daddy hate to leave town even more.

When David heard that Daddy was leaving for a two-week rest in the mountains that July, he noticed his concerned look and said, "Oh, don't worry about losing anyone in your congregation to my church while you are gone. I'll tell you what I'll do. I will mail you a package containing golf balls as a sign of what is happening back at home. If the balls are shiny and new it means that I have taken one of your good members. If the balls are old and dirty, it means I have gotten a member who was not that active anyway."

To this day I'm not sure that this plan pacified Daddy, but he did go to Montreat to rest and to play golf with his friends Billy and Jack. After a few days he went to the local post office to pick up mail and found a box mailed from David in Mobile. There was no note in the package but in it were two shiny golf balls on cotton backing. Daddy could not study in the Montreat library anymore. He headed to Mobile to his church. Upon arriving, he discovered that David had pulled a fast one. When he called David, his friend said, "That was just a joke. Your members are all intact. You didn't lose even one. I was just teasing." It was some years before Daddy ever took another vacation, but he was a forgiving man and played golf with David the very next week!

Daddy had fallen deeply in love with Mama when he was at Seminary in Richmond where she was at a Christian educator's training school across the street. He had gazed at her from a distance and admired her beauty, but had not met her officially. One Sunday morning he took the bus across town to a small church in the suburbs of Richmond where he was doing his "practice preaching." At the next bus stop the beautiful brown-eyed brunette, who had so caught his eye, boarded the same bus—an *empty* bus except for Daddy and the driver. Startled and surprised by the sudden approach of the object of his dreams, he quickly stood up and gave her his seat on the empty bus. This was the beginning of Chet and Betty as a couple.

Once Daddy fell in love he stayed in love. He courted Mom during their school years in Richmond until he asked her to marry him and go to a pretty little West Virginia town to join him in his first pastorate. She was bent on using her two years of training for work in Knoxville. After a year of work that must have been very difficult, the idea of marriage must have at last appealed to her. So Mama now said "Yes" to Daddy. He borrowed a ring from his best friend's sister for the wedding. He did not want to take a chance on buying a ring and having Mama change her mind. They had just experienced the Great Depression. His best friend, Jack, who was later a well-known minister and writer, gave the bride away in his first church in Farmville, Virginia.

Daddy and his golfing friend from Montreat, Billy, at our Mobile, Alabama home.

After the wedding and the honeymoon, when Mama had arrived with Daddy in the little West Virginia mountain town, she was wandering around the large two-storied manse, trying to immerse herself in the life of a minister's wife. She came downstairs on Saturday evening as he was working on his first sermon since the honeymoon and asked him what text he was preaching on the next morning. He looked up at her with a twinkle in his eye and replied, "I'm taking my text from the words of King Saul. 'I have sinned, I have played the fool, I have erred exceedingly!'"

She answered back without hesitation, "Well, Brother, you may have, but you are not going to tell the congregation that!"

Daddy and the Cod Liver Oil

"Better is a dinner of herbs where love is, than a stalled ox and hatred therewith."

—*Proverbs 15:17*

As I said earlier, there were hard times in the country after the Great Depression of the 1930's and the families of ministers had to make the money stretch. Sometimes the stretching was too much. I remember this day as clearly as I remember the day that President Kennedy was shot. Daddy came home from the drug store with vitamins and two large bottles of oils: cod liver oil and castor oil. The latter is what we were given when a switch wouldn't work as punishment. The cod liver oil was for our health. Daddy was proud that he had gotten such a large bottle for a good price even if it would take months to use it up. We were all standing in the kitchen and one of us accidentally knocked over the cod liver oil on the counter. The thick, golden liquid covered the whole top of the counter and some of it dribbled to the floor. Daddy was horrified to see his hard-earned money gone forever. He reached for the loaf of bread he had just bought and taking one piece of bread after another, he sopped up all the cod liver oil and gave each one of us a golden oiled piece of bread. It was probably the one time that each of us didn't fuss that the other was getting the largest piece. Every time I go to an Italian restaurant and they bring out loaves of fresh bread and a plate of oil, I am reminded of that time of cod liver oil and bread. Now, as a consequence, I always request butter instead of the oil, to the chagrin of the waitresses.

Daddy and Jane on the steps of the church.

On one of the last days of Daddy's life (he died at the age of 53), he took Mama's hand in his, looked deeply into her brown eyes and said, "You would have driven anyone else crazy, but you're all I ever wanted!"

As a child I was always trying to please Daddy. I wanted to look like a grownup so I would dress up in Mama's dresses and think I was fooling people. So, while I was in college, I wrote the following poem and submitted it to a National Poetry Contest, judged by Randall Jarrell, poet laureate of the U.S. in the 50's. It won 2nd place. He said, "This is just right about children."

UNRECOGNIZED

Why must I be like me
She thought as she trailed her Mother's gown?
What is a man's woman?
She'd heard Papa call her mother that—
Crinkling up her nose, she made a face.
A lovely woman you are,
She said as she gazed into the glass…
Lovely, beautiful all in black.
A man's woman must dress in
All red and black.
Yes, and have a look like this,
The darks of her eyes grew large,
Her spotted red lips puckered.
She must not wear blue socks.
Quickly she sat down
Within the rich black, veiling chiffon
And pulled off the thick wool socks.
I am a lady now, she thought.
Footsteps came into the hall.
It was a man.
He came and ruffled up her curls,
"Hello, my child."
She turned away—
Her father knew her not.

Childhood

"When I was a child, I talked like a child, thought like a child. When I became a man I put childish ways behind me. Now we see but a poor reflection as in a mirror: then we shall see face to face. Now I know in part, then I shall know fully, even as I am fully known."

—I Corinthians 13:11

Childhood was a time when days were long and lazy. I'm sure it was hot in the little town in Mississippi where I lived. If it was hot I didn't know it for I was busy running around barefooted in cotton sleeveless dresses and blonde hair tied up in two wisps with ribbons. Ella May was my mother's helper with household jobs and with the children. She would tell me to write letters to Santa at Christmas and to tell him what I wanted. She insisted that I put the letter in the big black stove through the round hole and the letter would go up to Santa through the chimney. Even at the age of four I thought that would be a dumb thing to do for surely the letter would burn up. However, I had a very strong desire to do whatever my elders asked of me so I did.

When I was a very young child, Mama instilled in me the certain knowledge that God was always present. He became a personal friend to me as a child and stayed that way throughout my life. I turned to Him for everything and it was a non-stop communion. At the age of three when I was sitting at a little white table with other young friends, my mother was passing out the napkins and I was noticed throwing my napkin up in the air. When questioned as to why, I answered, "I am throwing my napkin to Jesus. You forgot to give Him a napkin." Another time I remember being carried in Daddy's arms down the walk from the church and yelling, "Goodbye, Jesus. I'll see you next Sunday." Daddy used that illustration in a sermon saying how so many of us go to church and worship God while at church but forget to talk to Him the rest of the week.

My awareness of God has been strong all my life but unlike Mama, I was guilty of not talking about Him as much as I should. I pretty much took it for granted that almost everyone who I knew felt the same way. God was so personal to me that I talked to Him when I was walking, exercising, driving or in bed. There has always been a direct and ongoing communication. It always bothered me that some people felt they had to ask priests or Mary to intercede for them when one could go right straight to God and talk. I always pictured "my" Jesus dressed in sandals and rough sewn robe, gathering people around Him on the ground and traveling in an old fisherman's boat or walking miles from place to place and talking to His friends. He was never unreachable to me.

Jane at the age of two—in all her innocence.

ACCEPTED BY GOD

I am accepted by God!
All the facts of my life
Are a "yes" to Him?
Because I have asked to be accepted
And forgiven.
He does not turn away now saying,
"You have failed me!"
He understands as I confess my deepest guilt
And the longing of my heart,
As the tears fall hot and ugly
Down my mournful face.
He does not say, "How weak she is."
He loves me in spite of my failures.
He knows that I am His
And that I am filled with the building blocks
Of His perfect creation!
My genes are both weak and strong
And He accepts me
For all that I am.
I am made weak with faulty genes
So that I need Him completely.
He accepts me although I have failed to obey.
I have turned to Him in all His caring
And He has accepted me.
His word is,
"I love you!"

The Smallest Gift

"This is my commandment: Love each other."

—John 15:17

"Jesus said, 'Let the little children come to me, and do not hinder them, for the kingdom of heaven belongs to such as these.'"

—Matthew 19:14

In Mississippi at the manse (the home of the Presbyterian minister), ladies from the church visited us a great deal. I was so shy and afraid of people that I would run and hide either under the house in the cool, damp, red mud, or I would hide behind the sofa so I wouldn't have to talk to the visitors but would still be privileged to hear Mama tell her stories. The guests and I were both enthralled at her renditions of experiences. I hated for the guests to leave for when they were there Mama told the best stories.

In the small town of Starkville, Mississippi, there was a local taxi driver who would stop by to see Mama and Daddy and listen to her stories and Daddy's jokes. If he wasn't busy, he would squire me around town when I was three or four years old and show me his favorite places to go: the college, the lake, and the ice house where he would joke with friends. When I was a few years older there was a big old wagon with an old black man driving a lazy horse through town. From time to time I would hitch a ride to school as the driver made his rounds delivering wood, coal, and ice.

Most of my memories of childhood are happy ones. However, there were a few incidents that haunted me all of my life. As a result of these memories, my concern about the underdog has always been a fervent one.

Close to our small town there was a large cotton mill. The children of a few of the workers attended our schools and played in our neighborhood after school and on weekends. I remember clearly that a truckload of brothers and sisters with uncombed hair, ragged clothes and bare feet pulled up to the elementary school on our first day there. One boy on the truck had a wooden leg. As these children climbed down timidly off the truck, they were immediately surrounded by dozens of other children who clasped hands and made a circle around them, taunting and mocking them. I was only six but my heart hurt badly at the sight. I ran headlong into the circle, hitting the mockers and crying as I pummeled them. I, in turn was attacked, but it didn't matter as I got my point across.

One afternoon sometime later, I was playing across the street from my house with my neighborhood friends and also playing with one little tow-headed, barefooted girl who was visiting from the cotton mill. A neighborhood child of about five years, from a wealthy (as a child I always imagined people to be wealthy if they had Kleenex and Jergens Lotion in their bathrooms) family two blocks away, came by and said, "Come to my sixth birthday party on Saturday." As she seemed to address us all, three of us arrived at her house on Saturday with brightly colored boxes tied in shiny satin ribbons. The fourth child, from the mill, also came. I was behind the little barefoot girl. She was carrying a small, unwrapped cardboard box such as earrings come in. The birthday girl stopped this shy little tow head before she could reach the front door and said, "I didn't invite you to my party!" and turned her away. The little girl from the cotton mill turned away with tears in her eyes, and as she was turning thrust her present into the birthday girl's hand and said, "But I brought you a present." The birthday girl opened the box. Nested in a piece of cotton was a shiny ten cent piece. The birthday girl threw the box on the ground and said, "That's not a present!"

I have felt many pains in my life, but this one tears through my memory of childhood as a bomb that rips a building apart. It was the kind of cruelty that we see in many of the news stories in our world. Only God has been able to give me peace from this cruelty that I observed to this little child.

Discipline

o o o o o o o o o o o o o o o o o o o o o o o o o o o o o o o o o o
"A fool despises his father's instruction, but he who receives correction is prudent."

—*Proverbs 15:5*

Mama in the swing while Jane watches on the right.

Mama had unique ways to help us to learn to be better people. She begged me everyday to make my bed. She promised one day that if I went away to school without making my bed that she would surely call the principal and have her make me walk home and make the bed. It must have been very frustrating for her as a well-meaning mother who did not want me to follow in her genetic footsteps of disliking housework. At that time she didn't know much about genetics but she did know that the Bible said, "The sins of the father are visited upon the children…" I tested her with the unmade bed until at last she could take no more. I was at junior high during a Latin class when I heard over the public address system that "Jane Frist's mother called and she says that she is to walk home and to make her bed." I thought, "Sure, sure," at that comment. It was a two-mile walk. How Mama ever talked the principal into doing anything so embarrassing for one of her pupils I will never know. However, Mama had a way of approaching people with words that had power over them. I imagined she approached the principal by saying, "Miss Smith, you and I have talked in the past about how important discipline is and how important that it is to follow through when one has made a commitment with one's children. I have told Jane that if she doesn't make her bed, I will call her to walk home to make the bed. I think that her embarrassment about this incident will make her never forget and she will learn to be neat." I walked home so embarrassed that I didn't ever want to go back to school. To this day I hate to make the bed every day, and I still hate to clean house. Another punishment she had was to charge us 5 cents from our allowance for each belonging that we left out of place. One sock was 5 cents and two socks were 10 cents. This was her punishment for a while until she realized that she hated the heavy bookkeeping more than the messy home.

One of her most unusual punishments for her children was the following: when two sisters were having a strong disagreement, she would make them stand opposite each other on each side of a glass entrance door. They had to stare at each other until they laughed or forgave each other. They could not leave the door until they said that they were sorry and made peace with each other. It is too bad that her creative ways to stop "wars" would not work in today's world.

"Children obey your parents in the Lord, for this is right. Honor your father and mother which is the first commandment with a promise—"that it may go well with you and that you may enjoy long life on the earth."

—*Ephesians 6:1–3*

A "GROAN" EXPERIENCE

One day when I was little,
I decided to be big
And see how all the grown folks live
By putting on a wig.
I dressed in Papa's great long coat,
I climbed into his shoes,
I sprayed perfume into my hair
And read the daily news.
I wandered down the streets of town
To see what Papa sees.
I nodded to the folks and all
And bowed straight at the knees.
I stopped for coffee at a shop
And smoked a pipe, in fact,
I even went to meetings
'Cause there's where grown-ups act.
The whole day long I went about
And did like Papa did
So I speak from real experience
When I say,
"I'd rather be a kid!"

Jane with her first dog, Kayo.

Childhood—Kindergarten

"When I was a child, I spake as a child, I understood as a child: but when I became a man, I put away childish things."

—*I Corinthians 13:11*

When I was five years old, my first day of kindergarten was one of surprise and dismay. The kind of rules that were laid down didn't appear to me to fit in with the world that I knew. Here, one could only go to the bathroom at limited times. When you went out of the room, if someone took the chair in which you had been sitting, it was his or hers now. Another child could take the crayon that you had just put down. He could color his picture while you waited, in spite of the fact that you needed it more than he did. At least that is what I thought. We all had to take a thirty minute rest on the blanket on a hard floor lying next to all of the children who were strangers to one another.

On that day it wasn't long before I couldn't bear all the rules, and so, during rest time, I walked downstairs and out of the kindergarten room while the teacher was in another room. The kindergarten was in a building facing one of the busiest streets in town, the one leading from my Daddy's church and my house toward Mississippi State College, two miles away. The kindergarten was close to the college. I skipped along the sidewalk and headed back to town, glad I had left that miserable place and certain that I knew the way back home. After all, I had driven hundreds of miles with either Daddy or the taxi driver through that small town. Also, my parents had let me travel in a bus across the state by myself so I didn't understand why it was such a big deal that I had left the kindergarten. I found out that it was a big deal when the teacher called Mama and told her I was missing. Perhaps my determination not to be one of a group who all had to do the same thing still haunts me today for I cannot make up my mind to join a retirement home even when everyone says how he or she loves it. I'm thinking that retirement home togetherness must be a lot like the group togetherness in the kindgergarten.

My awareness of genetics kicks in as I think of another family member, my cousin Julie, who went to kindergarten the first day and decided she also hated going there with the other children. She, too, was the oldest child in her family and was not accustomed to conforming to every rule. She hated the class so much that she went to the principal's office and told the principal that her mother had told her to call a taxi and come home. Unlike our family, the preacher's family, she was accustomed to riding in taxis with her mother. The principal called the taxi. It took off with the little girl. Her mother couldn't believe it when she saw a taxi pull up to the front of her Orlando home and saw the black curly top of her daughter's hair sticking just above the window in the back seat. Julie jumped out and shouted, "Mom, please pay the taxi man. I told him you would."

Jane at kindergarten age with Daddy and sister Charlotte.

Contact Lenses

o o o o o o o o o o o o o o o o o o o o o o o o o o o o o o o o

"Listen, my son, to your father's instruction and do not forsake your mother's teaching. They will be a garland to grace your head and a chain to adorn your neck."

—*Proverbs. 1:8*

From the time I was nine years old and suddenly couldn't read the blackboard, I had to wear glasses. This tragedy became one of the worst things in my life. I prayed for fifty-seven years to get rid of them. I had disobeyed Mama and God in my mind in the instances where I read books with a flashlight under my bed when I had the measles. I didn't think that Mama knew what she was talking about when she said that it was dangerous and might hurt my eyes. I disobeyed Mama on that count and disobeyed God in that I didn't honor my mother in this situation. Therefore, when I became almost blind, I felt that I was being punished by God. It was agony to be a tall, skinny girl with glasses that often rusted on your face in the rain, and braces that made you look like a construction site. Children called me "four eyes." When you think you are ugly as a child, no amount of compliments when you grow up will ever take the early memories away! It is always a calming experience when one reads that nearly every child has some degrading experience like mine. It was in God's grace that my Mama, when she was close to death, took my face in her hands and said, "Why, Honey, you are so pretty." I never remembered her saying that to me before.

As I got older and it was time to date, Mama was so determined to help me change my image and blindness that she said that she would scrub floors in order for me to take off those "ugly glasses." Taking off the glasses meant that Mama and Dad stretched and bought me one of the first pair of contact lenses in the South. I drove all the way from Mobile to Atlanta to get them. At that time they were large oblong pieces of glass that one filled with distilled water and then took a rubber stopper with a suction cup and stuck the contacts in the eye, trying not to spill the water. The effect was unusual. Certain boys would tell me that my eyes were like "deep blue pools of water." I thought to myself, "They are."

When one would have to take off the lenses after less than two hours, the lights in every place around you had rainbows and then you were blind again. If two hours had passed and the contacts were off, your eyes would be red and if you had to go to the Ladies' Room, you never could find your date again. I would have died rather than put on my glasses. I lost quite a few dates that way.

PRAYER

Last night as I knelt beside my bed
With open heart and bowed head,
I felt that God was by my side.
He'd promised always to be my guide.
I knew that He was near
So I prayed in silence
Believing that He would hear.
I poured out my troubles
As one only would
Who prayed to a Father
She knew understood.
My worries and burdens were lifted and shared
With my Father above who loved me and cared.
Though no answer was spoken aloud as I knelt
In some way my prayers would be answered, I felt!
God always answers if one earnestly prays
Sometimes it takes years and often just a day
Though it may not be the answer we sought
God will say, "Yes, no or wait" if we pray as He taught.

The Answer to Prayer

○ ○

"Jesus asked him, 'What do you want me to do for you?'" "Lord, I want to see," he replied. Jesus said to him, 'Receive your sight. Your faith has healed you.'"

—Luke 8:41–42

After 55 years of wearing glasses and contacts and being almost blind, one of the many miracles of my life took place. Mother and I both had prayed for this miracle for many years, believing the prayer would be answered, but not believing also. "I believe, help my unbelief" says the verse in the Bible. Having contacts was part of the answer to getting rid of glasses. However, the other half was about to happen. Mother was, unfortunately, not on earth to witness this miracle, which was not unlike a biblical miracle where Jesus moistened clay, put it on the eyes of the blind man and then he could see.

When I heard about the new Lasik eye operations for near-sightedness, I wanted to have that operation but they were too costly and not always successful at first. One of my Montreat friends had the operation early on and her vision was made worse. I waited for quite a few years, thought about it, and worried that I would totally lose my vision. With my luck in life, it could be a guarantee that it wouldn't work out. It took a great leap of faith to decide to do it. I was tired of feeling my way along the halls to the bathroom at night; having broken glasses repaired and lost lenses retrieved. I was weary of conjunctivitis and sore eyes.

My sister traveled with me to the town where an ophthalmologist who had successfully completed ten thousand operations had his practice. It was comforting to have my sister share this amazing time with me. We were given free coffee after writing a check for $4,800.00 and told to sign papers and relax in a reclining chair. There were about fifteen other people all lying back in reclining chairs in the waiting room, no doubt lying back with their hearts pumping madly in fear. It was time to talk again to God and ask for His peace and presence. One by one each person's name was called and she or he left our room of safety and walked into the unknown. One had to desire ones sight back in an intense way in order to take this chance of having sight or blindness. A lot of taking this chance depended on having faith. The blind man in the Bible whom Jesus healed had that kind of faith.

When I was called in and told by the doctor to lie down on the operating table. I was then asked by him to look straight up at a strong red light that shown above me. He touched my eyes briefly with a laser stick. Nothing hurt at all. Within minutes I was asked by the doctor to stand up and look around. I was stunned that I could see clearly. I responded to him in a loud voice of joy and affirmation saying, "I was blind and now I see!" (John 9:25) The old familiar words of the Bible popped out in my mind.

The doctor answered, "Go and tell everyone!" I am pretty sure that Jesus was trying to keep his miracles quiet for a while and said, "Go and tell no one!" However, in this case, the doctor was happy to add one more name to those of the ten thousand other success stories and knew I would help him add a hundred more new clients with my newborn enthusiasm.

God does answer prayer. We've always been told that He doesn't always say "Yes", that He sometimes says "No" and last of all "Wait. Your time is not my time." That was one time when I waited! But what an answer! A dream come true. A pure miracle.

Prep School

o o o o o o o o o o o o o o o o o o o o o o o o o o o o o o o o o o

"My heart panteth, my strength faileth me: as for the light of mine eyes, it is also gone from me."

—*Psalm 38:10*

Those days of living with contact lenses and braces on my teeth were very difficult for me. Mama was less than pleased to have a teenager who didn't make her bed, who studied and read all the time and who did not look cute like her Mama wanted her to look. Even Mama, in her book *No Wings in the Manse*, writes of her opinion of me at the time: "For a while our child was quite scenic—or so we thought. Then she began to change. Adolescence set in, and though I have never told her so, it was often difficult for me, even, to look upon her without a mild shudder. We had to glass in her eyes at an early age; we had to put her teeth in splints; she shot up so fast that she seemed to sway a little at the top." Mama couldn't stomach teenagers so each of her four children was sent off to prep school.

I went to Peace College in Raleigh for high school. There is where my joy in living really began. I broke loose and started to be my own person. Not until after my marriage was over, however, did I begin to really bloom and make my own decisions. Before that, my strong Mama and my forceful husband insisted on making my decisions.

39

It seemed like everyone was pointing at Jane when she donned her first
pair of glasses.

In prep school I was matched with a roommate, Mary, who became my lifelong friend. In our last fifteen years, we have lived only two doors away from each
other in the mountains. An odd combination we were, five feet and nine inches
walking hand and hand with five feet and no inches. They called us "Mutt and
Jeff." We established a similar set of values in those days. Most of those values
have not changed in fifty-nine years. At fifteen we were full of mischief and tried
to get away with breaking what we thought were ridiculous rules. We would both
think up a prank and go through with it and thoroughly enjoy carrying out the
prank. It was only after we were caught that I was campused or sent to the school
court for punishment. Mary was rarely punished because she looked like a tiny,
golden-haired angel. She was a whiz at looking innocent while something about
me looked guilty.

Once we made a mannequin of a man who looked so real that he frightened
us in the dark. We clothed him in jeans, a shirt and baseball cap. We made a face
with stockings and drew the eyes, nose and lips. We set the man on the bed of a
nervous old maid teacher and lay on the floor by our door to hear the screams of
fright as the encounter took place. There was only one problem with our plan.
We had used *my* towels and clothes to stuff the man and we forgot that *my*

nametags were sewn into the towels. Guess who was punished. It was not **Mary**. She got a big kick out of my being campused instead of her.

Jane and Mary at Peace College prep school.

She and I climbed out on the chapel roof to sunbathe when we got tired of going to a required chapel service every day. We got out of classes sometimes when I pulled the contact lenses trick on a very old, half-blind French teacher. As I talked about before, my contacts were large pieces of glass that I was supposed to fill with distilled water. However, in order to get out of class, I filled the water in the glass contact with red or green cake coloring and attached the small brown rubber suction to the glass once it was in my eye. The result was that I looked as if I had a serious problem with my eyes. The teacher told me to leave class and go for help at once. She sent Mary with me to take care of me. Mary was as happy as I was.

Sometimes we had to go to concerts that were long and boring, especially if the whole concert was a solo singer. This particular evening when Mary and I were yawning and stretching with boredom at the concert, I realized that another contact lenses incident with the red cake coloring and rubber stopper had yet to be tried on our chaperone. When I showed her the red glowing, swollen looking eye, she was so shocked that she called a taxi for me to return to the school for first aid. Mary kindly accompanied me in the taxi back to the school where we enjoyed a few hours of freedom before the rest of the schoolgirls returned. In our later years when my old log cabin was too cold in the winter and I would go to Florida in order to be warm, if I came home too early and if the house was cold, Mary still took care of me. She and her husband invited me to stay as a guest in her extra apartment in their ten bedroom, five bath home. I was a fortunate girl to have a lifelong friend like Mary.

Jane and Mary all grown up and still great friends.

OUR SPECIAL BABY

When we've been bragging quite a lot
To neighbors 'round our coffee pot
About our newest tiny tot,
She does just what she should not!

But when she coos and acts aware,
And when she makes a big fanfare,
It's sure to be the one affair
When only Pop and I are there!

Children and Their Wisdom

○ ○

"Jesus said, 'Be careful. Don't think these little children are worth nothing. I tell you that they have angels in heaven who are always with my Father in heaven.'"

—Matthew 18:10–11 (NCV)

When I was four years old, I remember that several different members of the church would try very hard to have me tell them about what it was like to live in the preacher's family. One lady asked whom I liked best, my mama or my daddy. I replied without hesitating, "I love my Daddy the most and I love my Mama the best!" That is the kind of understanding of people that children have that often leaves them in adulthood. In my particular line of work I would hope that some of that knowledge has remained with me.

When my sister Charlotte was born and I was taken to the hospital to see her, I looked up at Mama nursing the new baby and asked, "Which one has the milk and which one has the orange juice?" Right after this I was pushing the new baby in a buggy down the sidewalk and a lady came up to us and said, "What do you think of your little sister? Do you think she is pretty?" I answered, "She has a good face!" Intuitively, even as a three-year old, I thought she was a good person! Of course, she was pretty as well!

Jane and sister Charlotte kissing.

When my daughter Jane Alden was only three and a half years old, her youngest brother Rob was born. We had tried to explain the birds and bees to her. Quite a few friends came by to call on the family and to see the new baby. One afternoon the doorbell rang and my daughter ran down to open the door and welcome the company. The company was a single lady who was very prim and proper. As Jane Alden entertained the lady while I was getting dressed upstairs, I overheard her ask the lady, "Do you have a baby like we do?" "No, I'm afraid I don't have any children," she said. Jane Alden eagerly spoke up and informed her, "Don't worry. My Daddy has lots of seeds and he'll be glad to share them with you."

One son David had his own mind from the day he was brought from the hospital nursery. If he wanted something at the age of two and I would not give it to him immediately, he would say, "If you don't do dat, I will say darnit, I will frow a fit and I will spit." He questioned me all about God from the moment he could say the word "God." He never stopped questioning and eventually my answers were not his answers and that broke my heart. He left America at sixteen with money he had saved from his newspaper route. He disappeared to Kathmandu for six years and was found by a certain religious group who gathered up lonely and frightened children who were far away from their parents. David had left America when he had been in rebellion against his father. For years his former schoolmaster told me that he was dead. This teacher had consulted a soothsayer. He paid $100 to this man to get an answer about David's disappearance. Although I didn't believe in this soothsayer, it didn't stop me from being torn up inside from what he said. The man told him that my son had been bathing in the Ganges River in India and was swept away to his death. My last letter from my son had mentioned that he had recently been swimming in the Ganges River. Not long after this I received a package with my son's camera and visa and no return address.

For years I did not give up trying to find him. I consulted ambassadors and state departments. There was no word from anywhere about him. Years went by and I struggled in real estate to make a living. One had to be all smiles and confidant toward the public. Underneath the smiles I was in deep pain. David had written such loving and caring letters at first. He had seen a huge field of purple poppies in Italy and expressed to me that he wanted to send me the whole field. He had said I had given him a legacy of thinking independently and that he appreciated all that I had done for him. Now he was gone and had been gone for years. On a trip that I took to Israel in the 80's, I put a folded note between the cracks in the remaining wall of the old Temple. In the note I asked God to please return my son to me if it were His will. Within six months, my neighbors, Ruth and Bill, sent a fellow Christian from India to search monasteries in India. They were always helping people. This man had heard rumors about an American studying in a monastery with a certain religious group. This Christian man found David in Dharmsala, India. David eventually became disillusioned with the group and asked me for money to return to the States. I borrowed the money and within six months he was home. I had prayed six or seven years. Eventually my prayers were answered…but only in God's time.

I had prayed over and over again, "I believe, help my unbelief." (Mark 9:24).

David in Kathmandu.

Fired Up

"God is our refuge and strength, an ever present help in trouble...Therefore we will not fear."

—*Psalm 46:1, 2*

In my will I had asked to be cremated. However, since then I have changed my mind. After Mama was buried in a sweet little country cemetery near Montreat, I enjoyed going there so much, walking around and reading the names and texts on the stones and thinking about the friends who had graced this earth and were now at peace. I thought of how each had affected my life. When I heard that one person had six plots for sale for the same price as the cost of one plot, I decided to change my will and be buried there. Friends asked what I would do with the other plots. I responded that for that price I could even bury the dogs and my children there with me. The two dogs could each have a grave and then there would be a plot for each one of my children and for me.

Since I am afraid of fire, I wondered why I had ever even considered cremation. Even though I know it takes place after death, my terror of fire because of past fire affected my thinking tremendously. When I was six years old my mother left for town and asked me to give the male renter some matches so he could light the space heater in the room where he was renting in our home. Renters and weddings brought in an extra dollar here and there as salaries for ministers were very low. I looked at the matches and thought there were enough in the box for me to borrow a couple. The crispy fall leaves under the porch looked like they would burn and why I wanted to see them burn, I don't know. However, they burned so well that the flames were licking at the big white columns on the porch. Luckily the porch floor was brick. Though appearing dumb enough to start a fire, I was not totally dumb and used the wind-up phone to call the operator and tell her about the fire. When the firefighters arrived, and the neighbors called the church and alerted Dad and Mama, I hid in the upstairs blanket chest at the top of the stairs. I will never forget how Mama stormed through the house "looking for that kid." I was more afraid of the punishment than the fire.

The most memorable fire that haunted the memory of my whole childhood took place on Sunday afternoon when I was ten years old. Mama and Dad had left me in charge of the three younger children while they called on different people from Dad's congregation who were ill in the hospital. The Quiz Kids were on my favorite radio station. This was some years before television. Tommy, the new baby in our family, was lying in a crib next to me in the extra room on the first floor. I heard the pitter-patter of little feet on the stairs, up and down and up and down and didn't think much about it. The two other children were just playing I figured. Soon my sister, Charlotte, was screaming that there was a fire in my parents' room upstairs. I left the baby in the crib, ran upstairs to look, saw the side of the room on fire within and around the fireplace and outside wall.

Running downstairs, I swooped up Tommy with a blanket, took him out and put him under a tree where he would be safe, called to the neighbors to call the fire department and watch all the kids. To this day he laughs at the saying, "I saved your life." Johnny and Charlotte had disappeared. I ran upstairs again and began to throw my parents' clothes out of the window farthest from the fire. Then I ran into my bedroom and threw my piggy bank with all my savings out the window. Then I went downstairs and outdoors to find the children and the baby. All were safe! Soon the fire trucks arrived and the firemen put out the fire. My three year old brother, Johnny, had wanted to see if the make-believe logs and paper in the false fireplace would burn. They did!

One neighbor tried to call the hospital and alert Mama and Dad to the situation. However, it was not long before some of the church members who were on the Manse Committee heard about the fire and came to the house. I offered to give them a tour of the home and the devastation that amounted to one wall and one fireplace. The real devastation was caused by my agreeing to tour the members of the congregation through the home on Sunday afternoon when Mama had not been give a chance to clean.

When Mama came home and discovered this situation, she was a wreck. After all, Sunday mornings before teaching Sunday school and going to church, it is all a mother can do to fix breakfast, dress the children and herself and arrive at church by 9:00 AM, much less have time to clean the house. Mama didn't get over that event so we soon moved to a new church and manse and made a new start. It was Mama's decision, of course. The rest of us didn't want to leave Tampa.

Jane and Tommy after she saved him from the fire.

Ruth

o o o o o o o o o o o o o o o o o o o o o o o o o o o o o o o o o o o o o

"Use hospitality one to another without grudging."

—*I Peter 4:9*

For a good many years after Tommy introduced my mother to Ruth, they were very close, shopping for antiques and log cabins, enjoying the mountain pool at Ruth's home and sharing meals together. They both loved to tell funny stories, to laugh, to study the Bible and quote Bible verses. Having been brought up by ministers and missionaries, they knew the Bible and taught it to their children as well as to many others. Both had a handful of children who were influenced by their love of the Bible and the fun times they had together.

Mother loved to take Ruth's children in her little VW Bug for ice cream treats at Custard's Last Stand. They waited eagerly until she came to Montreat for the summer. From time to time each child got his or her turn to spend the night at Aunt Betty's little log cabin. My mother loved to make the children laugh and she would go so far as to dive in a mountainside pool owned by Ruth and Billy clothed in stockings, heels, silk dress, girdle and earrings. If she had been wearing a hat, she would have worn that into the pool as well.

One night after coming home from college, I was dressing to go out on a date. One of Ruth's children, Gigi, was spending the night with their "Aunt Betty." None of my brothers and sister was completely happy when Ruth's children got all of mother's attention. However, we enjoyed them also, and we put up with endless attention paid to them. They seemed to appreciate Mama more than we did, for we were the ones disciplined and not they. That was their mother's job.

As I was getting ready for my date, I was leaning over to fill my big glass contact lenses with distilled water when Gigi appeared in the doorway to my room. Gigi was a seven-year-old kid with a reputation as a little spitfire, full of life, creativity and gumption. Her family and friends never knew what she would think up to do next. At eleven years old she drove her family's jeep down the mountain, loaded with her brothers and sisters. Not having been given driving lessons, she turned it over as she slipped on a muddy spot on the mountain road. Luckily, no one was killed, and the wreck only broke one arm, that of Gigi's sister. Now let's go back to the story of Gigi, a visitor in our home.

Gigi in a moment of quiet.

I was startled, when putting the lenses into my eyes to hear Gigi announce that when my boyfriend came to pick me up for the date, that she was going to tell him that I wore thick, ugly glasses! She stated boldly, "You aren't pretty at all when you wear those glasses. I'm going to tell your boy friend that you wear glasses and then he won't marry you." By now, impatient with Gigi, who had already taken over the house for more than half a day, I shot back, "If you do that, you little brat, I won't let you ever come to our house to spend the night again." Rushing into my room, Gigi picked up my glasses from the table and threw them at the stone fireplace in the living room, shouting, "You Red Devil, you!" The glasses were so thick that they just bounced and fell unbroken to the floor. Believe it or not, when Gigi and I grew up we became very close friends, just as her mom and my mom had been before us. We spent hours together going over passages in the Bible and discussing their meaning. We shopped together at antique and consignment shops. We often traveled together when she was asked to make speeches nearby. The worst thing that Gigi ever said to me as a grownup was, "When a room in Jane's house needs cleaning, she just builds on another room." Housecleaning was never one of my favorite chores but building was. I was forever adding a room or a porch to the tiny 800 square foot log cabin that I had bought from my Mama. The family teased me about all the "add-on" rooms in the cabin and called it "The house that Jane built!" One day my son Rob opened the door of my bathroom cabinet and exclaimed, "Mercy, here is another wing that I have never seen before!"

"A wife of noble character who can find? She is worth far more than rubies...She speaks with wisdom and faithful instruction is on her tongue."

—*Proverbs 31:10, 26*

Ruth.

For me, Ruth epitomized the perfect woman. She was not only beautiful, but she had a love of life that seemed unequaled. Her hazel eyes were always twinkling with another plan for making someone happier. She was also mischievous and her mind was always headed toward making someone laugh. There was sometimes a bit of shock that came with the deal. Once she came to our home right before dinner and announced to Mama that she had some fresh meat for dinner. She gave Tommy a brown bag and he brought it to Mama. Mama opened the bag and a black snake jumped out.

Another time she had promised a heavyset woman friend that she would help her with her diet. So when the friend was visiting and Ruth was making supper, she left off the whipped cream on one pecan pie, the dieter's pie, but put full swoops of whipped cream on the other pies. When her guest protested that she wanted Ruth to help her lose weight, but "please not tonight," Ruth told her to go back into the living room while she finished fixing the dinner. Ruth ran to the bathroom and retrieved her husband's shaving cream. With two big swooshes, Ruth adorned the bare pie. I wasn't there to hear the end of the story, but I am certain it was the last time that guest asked for help in dieting.

When Ruth was in her thirties, about the time she and Mama were just meeting, my brother Johnny came to visit our family and Ruth on his new motorcycle. Ruth was always seeking new adventures and she begged him to let her ride it. He at first objected, but after she gave him her winning smile and reassurances that she could handle the motorcycle, he helped her on. Off she went down the road to the next town, three miles away. When she decided that she had gone far enough, she realized Johnny had failed to teach her how to stop. She fell over in a field and a passing truck driver stopped to ask if he could help her. She asked him to just turn the motorcycle in the other direction and there would be someone at the other end to help her stop.

Once when she was hurrying home from town on the way to an important meeting and on the way to take a neighbor home, she was stopped by a State Trooper because she was speeding. When he began to write a ticket, she honestly and sweetly said, "Sir, it won't do any good to write a ticket as I will just have to break the speed limit again after I've left you as I am already late to a very important meeting. Also I have to take my passenger home first. However, if you will do me a favor and take this lady home for me, then I won't have to speed to get to this appointment." Can you believe that the Trooper did just that, never wrote up the first ticket and didn't have to write up a second ticket?! I believe that I heard that he really took the lady home so that Ruth was able to get to her meeting on time without speeding.

Gigi, Charlotte, Jane, Mama, Ruth and Tommy seeing Ruth off on train
in Black Mountain.

Coming Down the Mountain

Ruth was always thinking of others in the neighborhood. When one of her friends from childhood, P. D., was involved in a tragedy, the loss of her son in a car accident, Ruth invited her to come up to her guest room and stay for awhile, to find peace on top of the mountain. Ruth drove over to her friend's home to pick her up and bring her up the mountain. After winding up the hill, curve after curve, she came to the front of her log home and then slowed down and took off her seat belt. Instead of stepping on the brake, she absentmindedly gunned the accelerator! The car shot through the split rail fence and dropped 75 feet off the mountain. God must have been traveling with the two ladies. I believe he sent his angels to save his children from a certain death. The Volvo was slowed down in its descent by some small saplings and boulders. There were only a few shattered windows and bumps to show for this tremendous fall. Ruth had fallen across the seat onto her friend as she had just released her seat belt before accidentally accelerating the engine of the car. After realizing that the two of them had been miraculously saved with only a few bruises, Ruth pulled herself back onto her side of the car, turned to her friend and stated emphatically, "I told you I would help get your mind off your troubles, didn't I?"

There was a cell phone in the car so Ruth called for help. Two helpers were soon up in the parking lot, staring in amazement down the precipice to the fallen car. The two men slid on their seats down the mountain, pulled the ladies from the car and offered to slide further down to the bottom with the ladies on their backs. However, this offer was declined and the ladies slid on their own seats to the bottom by themselves. In later days, after the car was towed from it final resting place, a friend of Ruth gave her an authentic red and white STOP sign made and placed in the spot where the car had been, 75 feet down the steep hill.

Ruth believed the Bible when it said that the husband should lead the wife, but when her husband stated that after this accident she should not drive anymore, she was quick to answer from her Biblical knowledge: "I don't believe that I have read that Abraham ever told Sarah that she could not ride her camel anymore!"

After a friend, Mary Eleanor, and I had heard about this incident on the mountain, she and I gave a luncheon for Ruth, her friend, and her sister Virginia. We called it the "Thank God You Are Alive" party. I wrote a poem that was appropriate for the occasion. Mary Eleanor gathered her guitar in her arms and sang, "She'll Be Coming Down the Mountain when She Comes!" I had gone to the party store and bought black balloons with white writing which said, "Way, Way Over the Hill."

Ruth celebrates her 80th birthday with Gigi, Patricia and Andie.

WHAT A TRIP!

Swings in the trees, bikes on the ground,
Our Ruth has really been around!
One thing she had not tried as yet,
Was flying a silver Volvo jet!

She tried it just the other day,
When she and P.D. went to play.
Ruth wanted her to have some peace,
A time when troubles were to cease.

She took her to a get-away
Atop her mountain house to stay,
To rest and ponder quieter ways
To bring her breakfast on the trays.

When coming to a halt at four,
She shoved her foot onto the floor
Thinking she was slowing down
But really heading back to town!

The only thing, the way she drove
Was not approved yet at The Cove
She took a circumvented way,
"Amazing Grace" is what they say.

Flying through a wooden fence,
Didn't even make her wince,
And P.D. was caught up in this.
Neither one was really tense.

They flew through fence, through trees and sky,
Landing gently by and by.
We're sure God put His arms aloft
With tender love and touch so soft.

He cradled all within his hand,
And placed them softly on the land.
Up against a gentle tree,
Whole and live as they could be.

It's now we celebrate the day,
That they are here to laugh and pray.
That they are still alive at all,
That God reached out to break their fall!

Clarence

Mama met Clarence at a retirement home called Penny Farms many years after Daddy died. J. C. Penny built this retirement home in Florida not too far from Jacksonville in honor of his missionary parents. It is a lovely place with a golf course and cute old English buildings. I drove a moving van there from Orlando for Mama when she was ready to settle down in one place, have a place to store her furniture and travel. She never traveled after going there, as she was so happy with her life.

After several years there, Mama began a friendship with Clarence, someone who was like my father only in his sense of humor. His wife had been ill and unaware of the world around her for two years before her death. She had hardening of the arteries. One of Mama's volunteer services was to push her around the grounds of the retirement home in a wheelchair, as Clarence had been overwhelmed with the full care of her. When his wife died, Mama and numerous ladies fixed casseroles for him. When Mama took her casserole to him, she asked to be accompanied by a chaperone. We children never found out whether she really cooked that casserole or paid another lady to prepare it. All the single women of the retirement home perked up when Clarence came around. As he drove the church bus to a small church on Sunday nights and needed a pianist to go with him, a few of the single ladies began taking piano lessons. It was to their chagrin that Mama could play a fancy piano by ear and needed no lessons.

Mama and Clarence.

A year went by, a respectable time after the death of a spouse, when Clarence felt he could date. Mama was equally as careful to do the right thing as Clarence. They had both prayed a great deal about this next step. She waited a year and then they began to date. Their first date was a movie to see "Noah's Ark." I'm sure they took a chaperone to the movie with them. Even when I visited Mama I was called on to be a chaperone when she visited Clarence. Some years later when they married, nineteen years after Daddy had died, Mama told everyone that it was to be a "mixed marriage." She said that was because he was a Northerner and she was a Southerner. Clarence was from Long Island, New York. She also told everyone that they had decided not to have children. After all, he was in his 70's and she was in her late 60's. By the time he was eighty years old the family panicked when he drove. He rarely looked to the right or left when driving. He was sure God was taking care of him. We believed in God but when we rode with Clarence we usually screamed a lot.

AN ODE TO CLARENCE, MAMA'S 80 YEAR OLD HUSBAND

He drove a jeep in World War I
But then he drove with power!
He was recently arrested
Going 20 miles an hour!

He's slowly…slowly moving
In the fast lane of I-4
With a line of cars behind him,
Lined from Princeton down to Gore.

His eyes peer barely o'er the dash
His sight is dim with age
His foot lies loosely on the gas
He's got no brake or gage!

He travels parallel to one
Who's also going slow,
They lead a double line of cars
Going 30 or below!

Mama had one particular concern. Clarence already had bought a burial spot by his first wife. Mama solved that problem by buying a burial spot on the other side of his plot and making him promise to have his coffin tipped in her direction. Many years later after Clarence had died, Mama moved to North Carolina and her children buried her in Piney Grove Cemetery established in 1794 in Swannanoa, a beautiful spot near Montreat near her many friends and beloved mountains. My brother Tommy who knew how she liked unusual houses and surroundings, found a beautiful stone along a mountain road and had it moved to her place of rest, complete with the inscription: "Loved…Forgiven…At Peace." The stone would have pleased Mama, as it was not the kind of stone that graces many grave sites. It was more like the kinds of rustic stones seen on the graves in Switzerland near the Matterhorn. It was rustic like Mama's log cabins.

Her children rarely feel sad in approaching the grave since the stone causes us to smile broadly as we see it and remember her special individuality. My sister planted ivy at the foot of it that gives it a beauty not seen on graves where loved ones have put artificial flowers.

Mama's grave with her unusual tombstone.

Concerning death and funerals, I attended one funeral with my new cell phone, so new that I didn't know how to turn it off. I forgot that it was in my purse. The minister on the podium at the front of the church, standing between banks of flowers stated, "And then God called." At that very moment my phone rang and I nearly died of embarrassment as I struggled to turn it off. Not knowing how, I had to pull out the battery and go on as if nothing had happened. I am afraid that the peaceful aura of the funeral was disturbed.

A friend in our area, Teresa, tells the story of her relatives who lived way back in a mountain hollow. One of the cousins in the family died and the undertaker came to see that his body was prepared for viewing. The family bought him his first new suit and tie and he was placed in the coffin at his family home so that friends and other family could visit. The undertaker went away for the day and when he returned he noticed that his fine preparations of the deceased had been messed up. The dead man's hair was out of place, his tie and shirt and coat were rather bunched up and he looked totally askew. The undertaker asked what had happened to his work of art in the coffin. The family tried to explain. They said that after the undertaker had left the house, the family decided they had never been able to take a family portrait since all of the family had not been together at one time. So they hired a photographer, pulled the deceased out of the coffin and propped him up between the two largest men, on the front porch. It was difficult to keep him in that position for long. They had to be content to have a portrait where one member of the family had his eyes closed. Eventually they did obtain a once in a lifetime family portrait! There was only one problem. They could not get him back in the coffin exactly the way the undertaker had left him. In the end, the family got a picture and the undertaker probably received extra money for his trouble.

Martha

Martha was a beautiful young college girl and my Aunt Lucy's best friend when we lived in Starkville, near Mississippi State College. She was one of the college secretaries and for a short time she lived next door to us, rooming with a neighbor. She and my 22-year-old Aunt Lucy, who visited us from time to time, and would share evenings, giggling and eating snacks from Lucy's own snack closet in our kitchen. As a child of only six at that time, those two young college women fascinated me and I wanted to be just like them when I grew up. They had such charm and self-assurance and were always laughing! They let my sister and me tag along. They shared their treats with us. When Martha moved back to Greenville, Mississippi, I was devastated at the loss of her presence. She was like a second mother to me.

After she had been gone for quite a long time, I begged my parents to let me go and see her. I loved her as a small child loves a hero. She lived all the way across the state from where I lived, and Mama and Daddy were reluctant to let me go by myself. I reminded them that they allowed me to babysit my younger siblings. They felt they could trust me to do the right things. As a child I was very serious, quiet and dependable. However, in today's world it seems almost crazy to think that I traveled across the state by myself on a bus at the age of six. Perhaps the bus driver was supposed to take care of me. People did those things back in earlier days. When I arrived at Martha's home where she was living with her sister and parents, she entertained me for a whole week, taking me to a chimpanzee show and introducing me to her friends.

Some months after I returned home, we got a letter from Martha. We were thrilled to hear that she would be coming through Starkville on her way to Greenville on the train that came through town, only a block from our home.

She said that the train didn't stop in our town, but it would blow its whistle and then it would slow down as it came through town. She told Mom to bring her little six year old and three year old girls to wave to her when she came through town. We were to stand on the curb near the tracks and she would step out on the stairs and wave to us.

What an exciting day that was for us! My favorite friend in the world was coming to visit us again. We dressed in our best Sunday clothes and in our little black and white patent leather shoes and walked down the street just as we heard the long mournful whistle of the train, coming from way on the other side of town. Soon the train was slowing down in front of us, not for us to see Martha, but for the safety of the people in town. Martha had stepped down to the second step between two cars and was waving. Then she threw a big box toward us that landed and broke open not far from our feet! Martha and the train passed on out of sight before we knew it. We stooped to pick up the big cardboard box and the train took Martha on down the way and out of sight.

We excitedly tore into the box. Mama was almost more excited than we were. Inside was the gift of a lifetime for two little girls. The box was packed in white tissue that held two beautiful rose velveteen coats trimmed in white rabbit fur. When we arrived home and tried them on, they fit us perfectly. The package flying through the air to our feet must have excited us almost as much as when the Israelites reached up for the manna that fell from the heavens.

Jane and Charlotte at the age when they received coats from Martha.

Over the years we kept up with Martha, and she came to my wedding. We crossed paths again in future years when she came to visit her cousin, Tommy, who lived close to us in North Carolina. We heard many funny stories from Martha's sister and cousins about her escapades. One story is that when she was involved in The Garden Club of Greenville, the club was having their special yearly event and the speaker who was to be there was well known in the gardening world. The ladies were looking forward to her coming with great excitement! Martha, as chairman of the group, was informed that the speaker had been in a serious car wreck and couldn't come. Martha didn't want to disappoint the ladies so she didn't tell a single person that she had heard from the speaker and that she was not coming at all. On the day of the happening, Martha came to the event wrapped up from head to toe in white gauze and bandages. Her face and head were totally covered and she only had two small eyeholes. Climbing carefully and with an attendant's help, she ascended the stairs to the platform. She hobbled on crutches to the stage. She approached the speaker's podium and began to talk in a deep pitched voice, assuring the audience that even though she had been in a bad car wreck, they were so important to her that she had made a great effort to be here and not miss this occasion.

Her talk astounded the garden club. She suggested that they paint each of their homes the colors of their flowers in the yard, painting each side of the home a different color. She went on and on with other outrageous ideas until the initial murmuring of the ladies grew into a certain pandemonium. At that point, she began to unravel the bandages and appeared unbandaged. It was Martha, the club's president. She was laughing so hard that she nearly fell off the podium. I've always admired Martha for her ability to turn a calamity into a great occasion.

West Virginia Bound

"We…have joy with our troubles because we know that these troubles produce patience and patience produces character and character produces hope."

—Romans 5:3, 4

Every summer for quite a few years, our family would make the long trek from Mobile to Moorefield, West Virginia, where Daddy's first church had been and where I had spent the first two years of life. My parents had not forgotten the dear friends from their early ministry and longed to be back in that area for a few months every summer. Mama found an old, historical, brick Georgian home on a hill overlooking the beautiful Shenandoah Valley.

With Daddy's help she was able to purchase it for a song. Rumors had the house haunted, and so, apparently, no one else wanted it. Supposedly there had once been a murder on the winding steps leading from the upstairs hall to the lower hall. As the murder took place, so the story went, lightning struck the brick right in front of the staircase and the bricks showed a jagged crack from the second floor to the first floor. Mama didn't have any place for superstition in her thinking. If the price was right, then the house was right! The land on which the house stood was home to a tree where George Washington was supposed to have carved his initials when he had surveyed much of the land in this valley. Also on the land was an outside kitchen, a bit removed from the main house in case of fire. There was a wide and deep hole for ice taken from the ponds where straw was placed and food stored. There was a house for drying meat and an authentic three hole outhouse. There were no bathrooms in the house our first summer there. We felt like real pioneers. My sister and I would walk into town with a wagon to get a fifty pound block of ice and by the time we pulled the wagon up the hill and home, the distance of about a mile, the ice had melted down to about thirty-five pounds.

Driving all the way to West Virginia with parents, four children and Albert in the car was an awful ordeal. Albert was our cook and our helper in all areas of the house. The crowded car was an agony we all endured for three days because of the joy of arriving in the cool and beautiful Shenandoah Valley with its gentle blue saddleback mountains in the distance. In those days there was no air-conditioning nor radios with music to soothe one's soul. The windows were open for air whether the air was hot or bug-filled. Each of the children fought for his turn to sit by the one free window on the right back. Albert got to sit by the back left window, sipping his quart of coffee that never seemed to disappear. I think he also blew smoke from a cigar, but of that I am not totally sure. He certainly smoked cigars at home. The baby, Tommy, had the place of honor between Mama and Daddy on the front seat and all he had to do to obtain a response was to cry. If things got overwhelmingly unbearable, one of us children could ride in the trailer. The trailer was really a little peaked roof house on two wheels that was pulled behind a little 1946 blue Ford. Mama and Daddy called it a trailer but to everyone else it looked exactly like an outhouse on wheels. In it was a black and white striped straw mattress on the floor and a few suitcases that could not be packed in the trunk of the car. Though the trailer had no windows and was bouncy and uncomfortable, it was heaven to be the one who got to ride in it, lying on ones stomach and holding on to the mattress for dear life. Once it broke away from the car. We were fortunate at that time that no one was in the trailer. There were no laws then that we knew of that said one couldn't ride in a trailer towed behind a car. Mama needed the trailer for her summer collections of old antique furniture that the mountain people didn't want. As I said before, many mountain people as well as people in general felt that new from Sears was much better than old antique furniture that often sat falling apart on an outdoor porch.

College: Robert Frost

o o o o o o o o o o o o o o o o o o o o o o o o o o o o o o

"Do not worry about anything, but pray and ask God for everything you need, always giving thanks, and God's peace which is so great we cannot understand it, will keep your hearts and minds in Christ Jesus."

—*Philippians 4:6, 7*

Famous authors such as Robert Frost and Catherine Marshall often came for a special day or weekend at Agnes Scott College in the 1950's. They would speak in our chapel from the stage and then the students were invited to meet these great people at a reception. I was in charge of setting up the reception several times during these yearly visits. Because I was an English major and loved to read in general, this was a very exciting time for me.

During one of Robert Frost's visits, I bought his book of poetry and asked him to sign it for me. He teasingly wrote, "To Frist from Frost" in the front of the book, along with his whole signature. I was so crazy about his poems and so delighted with his signature in my book, that I protected it carefully over the years.

When I first arrived in Florida from Denver, I had to store a lot of furnishings and books since I had rented an apartment rather than buying a home. It is often difficult to start a new business in a new area. I was in real estate and knew so few people that my income was low. Soon, I couldn't afford to pay high storage rental costs so I commandeered my cousin, Julie, to help me sell some of the stuff. She moved lots of items to her carport and had a garage sale for days on end. I was rarely there because I was working.

One day she came to me, delighted that she had made $15.00 on the sale of a whole box of books. Suddenly terror struck at my heart as I realized that I had forgotten to look through the books and to save my favorites. The main book about which I was concerned was the volume by Robert Frost. I questioned her frantically about who the book dealer was who bought the books. She didn't remember any name or where he was from. It took me a long time to get over that loss and move on.

Some seven years later I headed for my dentist in Winter Park, Florida. The offices were arranged side-by-side opening to an outdoor corridor. As I walked down its length to the last office in the complex, I heard footsteps behind me and they seemed to be going exactly where I was going.

After entering the office and signing my name at the secretary's window, I looked around and saw that I was the only one in the office other than the man coming in behind me. "Good, I won't have to wait long," I thought to myself. I picked up a magazine and started to read. However, I noticed that the patient who entered the door after me was perusing the sign-in pad for a bit longer than one normally would. He looked over at me with a funny look on his face and then rather than taking a seat across the room, he came straight to my chair and stood in front of me.

"To Frist from Frost" he stated! I stared at him, rather startled at his words. He repeated the same words. My face turned red as I realized something unspoken as yet. "You know about my Robert Frost book!" I said eagerly, hoping he did know where it was but not having any idea why he would know about it.

"May I sit here next to you and tell you a story? By the way my name is Bill Watson and is yours Frist?" He pulled one of the office chairs beside mine and continued to talk to me. I noticed that he had a rich, deep voice somewhat like my radio announcer cousin had. I was not surprised to hear him say, "I am a radio announcer in the area and have been here for many years. Although I am sixty years old, I recently got married to a lovely young woman and one of my wedding presents was Robert Frost's book of poetry." Still curious about my book and wondering where this story was going, I got a bit impatient and started to interrupt him but didn't as he seemed enthralled himself with the story he was telling me.

"My brother lives in South Florida and was looking for a special gift for me for the wedding. Among other stores, he was perusing a second hand gift shop. He found this Robert Frost book and knowing that Frost is one of my favorite poets he wrapped the book in silver paper and gave it to me. However, believe it or not, he never noticed Frost's signature in front. I noticed that on my honeymoon when I was reading poetry to my wife from the book. You must know that I was totally stunned! My older sister had graduated from Agnes Scott many years before. We visited my sister in Georgia while on our honeymoon. Once I told her about the book and about the inscription she asked to see the book and looked in the front and saw the words, 'Agnes Scott College' and the date of '1954' written there. She said, 'I can't imagine anyone letting go of this book signed by Robert Frost. If you ever find out who she was, you will have to give her back her book.'"

"'No way,' I answered her," he said. "'You know how over many years, I have memorized so many of his poems and now I have his own signature. It's now my book and it was bought by my brother just for me!'" At this point, he shook his head sadly and said, "Now that I have seen you, I know for a fact that I must give it back to you. But I want to make it a special occasion." He invited me to meet him and his new bride for dinner at a fine restaurant nearby and he said that he want to present me with my book.

When we were called into the separate rooms of the dentist office, I could hear him in the next room excitedly repeating the story to the dentist.

Within ten days we met together and he brought his attractive young wife along. After we were eating, he showed me how he could recite verse after verse without even looking at the book. Candlelight, seafood and wine made this evening very special. I was amazed at all he was doing for me. Then he presented me with a package wrapped in silver paper and ribbons. I opened it to find my old familiar green book, just about as worn as when I had owned it.

This is just another way that God takes care of me. No one can tell me any different. When God is involved, the emerging stories can be unique!

Some months later I was telling this story about the Robert Frost book of poetry at the Assembly Inn in my small town of Montreat. After telling the story, a visitor, a lady in her fifties or sixties at that time, announced that she had a story that she wanted to tell all of us. She began, "When I was at Chapel Hill, I was in one of the large English classes and we were studying poetry of Robert Frost. The professor read one of Robert Frost's poems. She then called on one of the girls in the class to interpret it. The girl stood up and gave her personal interpretation. The professor said, 'Contradictory to your thoughts on the poem, I am almost certain that Robert Frost meant the poem to say such and such,' and she gave her own interpretation. Suddenly from the back corner of the room, a very old, wrinkled white-haired man stood up. 'I am sorry to tell you this, Professor, but this young girl here has the correct understanding of the poem just as I meant it to be when I wrote it.' Robert Frost liked to show up uninvited to classes where his poetry was being taught and to see how his poetry was being interpreted. The class was vastly amused, and the professor was surprised and rather intimidated."

College: "A Man Called Peter"

o o o o o o o o o o o o o o o o o o o o o o o o o o o o o o o
"Everything is possible for him who believes."

—*Mark 9:23*

As I said before, during my years at Agnes Scott College several famous authors came during the year to talk about their books. Among these was Catherine Marshall. Catherine had been a student at college some years earlier and had married the Scottish preacher, Peter Marshall, whose sermons and books were well known at the time. His life story was thought to be worthy of a movie. All the girls at the school were thrilled to hear that the movie with the Hollywood cast would be made in the Atlanta area as well as at our college.

The big day arrived when the producer and director of the movie came to our campus in order to choose extras for the production. It was a hot fall day in Atlanta, but I decided to wear the brightest colors of clothing that I had in my closet. Unfortunately for my comfort, orange was the predominant color of a wool skirt and wool sweater that I decided to wear. I felt certain that the discomfort of a few hours would be worth suffering if I might be noticed and chosen to be an extra in the movie.

As it turned out, groups of girls gathered excitedly on the Quadrangle by the brick buildings and deep green foliage of the campus. We all wanted to attract the attention of the director. We either waved our hands when they asked who would like to be an extra or hoped that we would be noticed for some other reason. I was tall and thin and my hair was blonde. I stood taller than most of the other girls. "You, Queenie, back there on the last row, come up here." I slipped through the crowd of girls, thrilled that I was one of the ones chosen. It wasn't long before quite a few girls were chosen to be extras in the movie and different spots on the campus were chosen for background scenes. Later on, as the movie progressed, I was filmed along with numerous others in many scenes. I called home and, with tongue in cheek, I stated to my mama that I was playing second to Jean Peters, the star of the movie. I thought that the family understood what I was saying was just a joke but that statement was taken quite literally by Mama.

Weeks went by and the extras spent an inordinate amount of time being filmed and watching the filming. I don't think that many papers were written or books read during this time. We took turns walking through the Quadrangle as the camera rolled again and again, redoing earlier scenes. It was tiring for all of us. When the movie came out, at last, many months later, we all attended the theater with bated breath. There was no person in an orange outfit that I could find. I was naturally horribly disappointed. I figured I must not have looked closely so I bought another ticket and went to the theater again. Success! There was one quick scene where I was walking across the Quadrangle in an orange outfit with an armload of books right before Catherine goes to a Sunday vesper service in a truck with Peter Marshall. Years later when the film was shown on TV in the middle of the night, I would wake up my kids to see that fast flash of film where their mother had her movie debut. Needless to say, they were not happy.

Within days of the movie's opening, I called home to tell some more about the movie. Daddy spoke with great sternness and reserve. "Honey," he said, "your mother is too upset to talk to you. She invited a whole group of her friends to the movie. She then took them all out to lunch and told them that you were playing *second* to the leading lady. They said they could not find you anywhere in the movie!" He went on to say that this particular unfortunate incident was a second unfortunate happening concerning me and Mama. He stated that she might not be able to emotionally talk to me on the phone for some months to come because of the pain and embarrassment this whole thing had cost her. He continued, "Also, she just found her antique quilt with a hole the shape of an iron in it that you must have used to iron your clothes on the last time you were here." College days are when one makes mistakes over and over again and hopefully matures in the process. I have spent my life in that process.

"If we confess our sins, He is faithful and just to forgive us our sins and to cleanse us from all unrighteousness."

—I John 1:9

College: Miss Laney

"Whoever loves discipline loves knowledge, but he who hates correction is stupid."

—Proverbs 12:1

Miss Laney was known on campus as the Grand Dame of English. She inspired fear in the hearts of those who could not answer her questions immediately and she respected those who were able to raise their hands the fastest. I was terrified of her. It seemed that everything that I did irritated her a little bit more. She would call me "Miss First" rather than Frist (she called everyone by the wrong name and no one corrected her) with a tone of derision in her voice. No matter how hard I studied, it seemed I could never get the answer that she wanted nor phrase it the way she preferred.

I spent a lot of time trying to make up to her for my lack of knowledge of syntax. One day when she was struggling with a big plate glass window in the classroom, I rushed up to her and slammed it shut. She stared at me through her thick glasses with a disdainful look, somewhat like an angry dragon and snorted, "MISS FIRST, I was trying to open the window."

My next try for her acceptance came soon after this particular incident. It was a lovely spring day and I was walking along the sidewalk on the edge of the campus, when I noticed that Miss Laney was standing outside her house on her lawn, looking down at the mouth of the hose and shaking it. Water did not seem to be emerging. I rushed over and turned the handle on the faucet beside her. The water gushed forth from the hose right into her face. She sputtered and sputtered as I tried to explain to her that I was just trying to help her. I do not remember what her words to me that day were, but I still shake when I think back on that experience.

It is amazing to me that I ended up majoring in English, got my teaching certificate and taught third grade for years. I also wrote hundreds of poems and delighted in writing small children's books that I never sent off to be published. She had a strong influence on me. Perhaps to this day I am still trying to please her.

After college when I lived in Denver, I was married and had three children. One day I saw a funny black 1930s car just like the one Miss Laney had owned during our college years. This car was going very slowly and holding up traffic. As I passed the car, I noticed that there was an old lady driving behind the steering wheel, sitting up straight as a rail. She had on thick glasses. She wore a hairdo just like Miss Laney had worn some ten years before. Then I realized that the lady I had passed was the same one who had struck terror in my heart. I pulled to the side of the street and followed her home. She and I had a warm reunion. I ended up asking her over to my house for several meals. Her whole personality was different. To my surprise, she had dropped her strict ways and was playful with the children and very warm to me. Another friend, Louise, from my former college, was living in Denver and had also studied under Miss Laney. She and I cared for Miss Laney and visited her until the day she died. We would take casseroles and cakes to her and to her sister with whom she lived after she retired. One day when Louise called her and she didn't answer the phone, my friend rushed over and found her on the floor at the base of her reading lamp, dead, with a book in her hand. She was reading up to the very end.

College: The Georgia Tech Dance

"To everything there is a season…a time to laugh, a time to mourn, and a time to dance."

—*Ecclesiastes 3:1, 4*

Miss Laney announced that our big Sophomore English thesis was due on Saturday morning, just after the weekend fall dance at Georgia Tech. What an inconvenient time! I worked hard the week before so that the thesis would not hang over my head. It was completed early so that I had time to get my orchid shantung strapless evening dress ready for the Tech dance on that Friday night. At Agnes Scott in the 50s, a chaperone was needed to go to such a dance; alternatively one could stay at the home of an adult friend or family member. The minister of my church in Atlanta, Vernon, had been my father's classmate at seminary so when he was made aware of my need for a place to stay, he and his wife offered me their spare room for Friday night.

My date picked me up at the dorm on Friday afternoon and took me to my hosts' home in Atlanta where I visited for a while, ate dinner and then changed into my evening dress. Vernon, my host, gave me the key to the house. He emphasized that they liked to go to bed early so I was to use the key whenever I got in. The dance was great, and the late night extended into an even later night because the evening included an early morning breakfast. When I returned to the minister's house it was still dark. I couldn't find the key anywhere so I told my date that there was no way I was going to ring the doorbell and wake up my kind hosts. I said that I would sleep in the hosts' car. In those days people rarely locked cars, and I could see that the window was down and the door unlocked. My date protested but finally agreed to pick me up at about 7:00 AM so I could get my sophomore thesis in to Miss Laney on time. Class was at 8:00 AM.

I didn't want to wake up my hosts that early to tell them what had happened and to get my overnight case so I wore the purple evening dress and the purple orchid back to campus. My date drove me as close to my dorm as possible. Unfortunately, as I exited the car in my wrinkled strapless evening dress at 7:30 AM who should walk by me on the sidewalk but Miss Laney, my sophomore English teacher. She stopped in surprise as she stared at me from head to foot and said, "Miss First, you could be a good writer if you didn't take on so many extra curricular activities and spread yourself so thinly around the campus." I think she was talking about all the clubs in which I got involved such as BOZ, the writing club, the Christian Association, the swimming ballet group, the International Student group, Aurora, the college magazine and the May Day Dance group. Besides that, I enjoyed dating the young men at Emory, Georgia Tech and Columbia Seminary.

> *"Counsel is mine and sound wisdom. I am understanding; I have strength."*
>
> *—Proverbs 8:14*

> *"He that walketh with wise men shall be wise…*
>
> *—Proverbs 13:20*

Jane with her orchid given to her before the Georgia Tech dance.

MEMORIES OF STUDYING FOR MISS LANEY'S EXAM IN THE COLLEGE LIBRARY

Endless rows of tables
Scattered papers, open notebooks,
Pink faces and white faces,
Screwed up in thought,
Half asleep,
Red-faced, frantic!
Constant shifting of legs,
Bent, crossed legs, short stretched legs,
Hands nervously clutching pencils
Mouths chewing ruthlessly on gum.
Bitten fingernails and gnawed pencils,
Constant sounds of shifting papers,
Slamming of books, hurried writing.
Here a sniff, there a cough,
Clanking of ink bottles against the table,
Clomping of rain boots down the aisles,
Muffled laughter, razzing whispers,
Jerky erasure sounds, taps of heels,
Sound of shifting chairs,
Echoes of feet upstairs,
Hushed smooth constant purr of heat,
Sights of tall windows bordered by steel and cement
Scenes of flawless blue sky
Framed by fleeting birds and
Golden leaves dancing in the sun.
Brown leaves blowing in the cool, lusty air,
Sounds of nature muffled by thick walls,
Systematic click of an electric clock.
It's coming closer, closer, closer,

Hurry, study, learn.
Can't, can't…
More time…give me more time…
I must, I must, I must learn…
Hurry, hurry, hurry,
Too late.
It's here.
Exam!

Illustrating Mama's First Book

"If you need wisdom—if you want to know what God wants you to do—ask Him, and He will gladly tell you."

—James 1:5

At the end of my sophomore year in college, I was thrilled to be going to work in the Christian Ministry Program in the National Parks. My job was to work in art and advertising for the program and as the hostess in the dining hall at Old Faithful Lodge. My special job daily was to set the approximate time that Old Faithful would shoot into the sky. There was a wooden sign that stood near Old Faithful and I would change it according to when we hoped it would go off. We were not always correct because nature has its own ideas. I was to ride a bus with Stella, another Agnes Scott friend who would also work in this program. We were to ride overnight from North Carolina to Ohio and then meet up with a young college boy, Mummy, who was going to drive his car and share travel expenses all the way to Yellowstone. He had written us of an elaborate plan to tour the west including the Grand Canyon, Bryce Canyon, the Grand Tetons and other famous places on our way to Yellowstone. We planned to sleep on sleeping bags on the ground on nice nights and in the car on rainy or cold nights.

One night we slept in a wheat field and covered our suitcases with straw so no one would steal them. We did such an awesome job at hiding them that in the morning we drove off without our luggage. Many miles later we realized what we had done and we had to retrace our steps for miles back. Another night when we pulled up in the dark in a field with dry ditches, we placed our sleeping bags on the dry ground rather in the wheat fields. In the early morning we woke up in shock as the irrigation ditches where we were sleeping began to fill with water. After these two experiences we slept sitting up in the car.

Jane at Lake Susan before leaving for Yellowstone.

After college closed for the summer and before the trip west began, I stopped by Montreat for one day to see my family and my friends. As I arrived at the front door of our home, my heart beating from the excitement of seeing my beloved retreat again, Mama met me with eagerness in her voice and pleasure on her face! "You are just in time, Honey. My publisher called from New Jersey and they want you to draw eleven pictures for the book I just wrote called *No Wings in the Manse.* They need the pictures within the week. You can do it, Honey. It will be easy!"

I cried out in agony at the thought of not seeing my friends who I would probably not see again for another year if I didn't see them on this one day. "But, Mama, I want to see my friends and there is no way I can draw eleven pictures in one day."

She answered, "There is no other choice. You must do them. I have already bought some black India ink and white paper. I will tell you just what pictures I will need to illustrate each chapter. I will need a picture of a 1918 touring car and...." She went on and on as she described the eleven pictures I was to draw within a few hours.

"I can't, Mama. I have no idea what those cars looked like."

She answered, "Don't worry, Honey, I will describe it to you as you draw!" To make a long story short, the hours went by as I struggled to reproduce what was in *her* mind. After many weary hours my tears began to flow and they flowed right onto the black ink on several drawings, destroying what I had tried so hard to produce. Over and over I began reworking the many tear stained line drawings until at last Mama was satisfied. By now it was 7:00 PM My friend and I were slated to catch a 10:00 PM bus to Ohio that very night. We got to the station on time, leaving Montreat far behind. It wasn't until months later that I thought again of these line drawings. It was on the day of Mama's first autograph party.

Mama dealing with her children and a neighbor.

Mama's family on the way to Virginia.   Daddy's choir

The Trip to Europe

"Like cold water to a weary soul is good news from a distant land."

—*Proverbs 25:29*

By the age of twenty-two, I had attended graduate school and married. After my wedding, we headed for Europe and Germany where my husband had won a scholarship from Princeton Theological Seminary and the German government. He was to have a year abroad studying famous German theologians at Bonn University. We left on a boat, not a ship, from New York. Rather than walking up a gangplank, the boat was so small and insignificant that we walked down the gangplank. My friend, Ruth was in New York at the time and pleased us immensely by seeing us off.

To cross the Atlantic our boat took about ten days whereas most ships took five days. We were both poor students and could not afford the best accommodations. Our small stateroom was wedged in between the heating pipes and boiler room and the noise was incredible. The boat swerved and swayed and even ran through the middle of a whale, cutting it in half. That was the most interesting event on the trip.

We had to be very frugal as my husband shared his fellowship stipend with me for a full year. We had 75 cents a day for both of us for food. We ate bratwurst, sesame rolls, cheese and spinach. We drank bean coffee most mornings. Unfortunately, we never got to experience the fine European foods about which most tourists rave.

My husband was proud of his ability to speak German, having studied at the seminary during his off hours. When we were put off a train because he used a third class ticket on a first class train I discovered his German was only rudimentary. No wonder the coaches were so luxurious. The conductor noticed the discrepancy, and escorted us off the train. He pulled the emergency cord and made sure we departed the train.

Standing sheepishly by the empty tracks with our suitcases, we realized that we had quite a long walk back to the small village that the train had passed. After the trek back, we went to a little outdoor café where my husband ordered for us in the German that he thought he knew. The result was we received food that was totally different from what we thought we ordered. It was only enough for one person. That night when we found an old pock-marked hotel, the damage having been left over from the war, we decided if it looked that bad on the outside, it must be inexpensive. It wasn't until we had gone to the room assigned, used the fresh white towels, rumpled the bed covers while resting, and entered the dining room that we saw the prices of the hotel written in English. It was about ten times more expensive than my husband had thought. We ran back to the room and checked out, having to pay only for a maid and the fresh towels we had used. I forgot to mention that the hotel manager was shaking his fist at us as we left the hotel.

I was by now deciding that my husband should certainly use his theological German only in classes at the University. I decided to enroll in a course in street German so we could order, buy and travel without embarrassment. I wanted no more being put off trains or being put out of hotels. However, one more embarrassing thing happened before I could enroll in the German course at Heidelberg University. Where we were renting, there was only one toilet for the whole house of young college students. Within that bathroom stood the toilet and a small sink. We were informed that if we wanted a bath, we would have to ride the bus to town to the bathhouse and carry our own soap, washcloth and towel.

My husband read on the sign at the bathhouse that the bathtub was the highest price, the shower the next most expensive and the pool was the cheapest of all. Unfortunately he read the sign incorrectly and purchased a ticket for what he thought was Men's Day at the pool. He went in and disrobed down to his birthday suit. He said that had been the custom at his particular California YMCA. After one day of hot and dirty train travel, he ran eagerly toward the pool. As he stood ready to dive in the pool, he noticed that women occupied the pool and not men. The women were all pointing at him and giggling. He had read the sign wrong again. It was Ladies' Day at the pool!

During our eighteen months living in Germany, we traveled around Europe during weekends and holidays, enjoying the small towns and their festivals, seeing great cathedrals and castles, and breathing in the beautiful scenery. We were able to travel many places. We stayed in Youth Hostels and hitchhiked. In those days college kids were doing that everywhere and there didn't seem to be any danger. In today's world, I shudder at the thought of taking such chances. Youth hostels were fun—we met people from all over the world and exchanged ideas with them as we ate our bratwurst and cheese in the common rooms. We learned where to go and what to see and what places were the most reasonable. One hardly needed a guidebook in those days. One day I looked up from the lower bunk in a youth hostel in Innsbruck and in the upper bunk was an Agnes Scott College friend. Another time, in Florence, right in front of Michelangelo's Pieta statue, we bumped into friends Nancy and Sam from Montreat.

The most memorable mode of travel happened one day in France when we had been standing on the side of the road for hours and no one was picking us up. Even then, France was known for its less than stellar treatment of Americans. It began to rain and then pour and still we stood, soaked to the skin and way out in the country. The French shot by us, never slowing down. After waiting six hours on the side of the road, an old farmer came along driving two big farm horses that looked like the Clydesdale horses. He was sitting on a bench in an old beer wagon that carried huge kegs of beer. It was near twilight so when he beckoned us to climb aboard, we did so eagerly. Even though I had studied French for five years, I could only understand a few of his words. It was enough to know that we were invited for the night at his centuries old farmhouse where the horses stayed on one side of the wall on the first floor and the guests on the other side of the wall. All night we could hear the horses kicking the wall and wetting the wall only inches away from our heads. After this experience we borrowed money and bought a VW bug. We shared gas costs with other students and often shared our single room with interesting friends we met along the way.

Several years later in 1967 when Apollo 1 exploded, killing astronauts Gus Grissom, Ed White and Roger Chaffee, we were watching TV in America and were amazed to see that one of the old friends who had slept on pallets on our floor in Bonn was the Chaplain who conducted the funeral service. He was now the chaplain at West Point. We were later to get together at West Point for a reunion with him and his wife.

Blue jeans were unknown to our landlady as to most Germans at the time. She shook her head and her fist at them, implying that they were indecent. Children often made fun our different clothes. My husband said that I should ignore the stares and remarks we often received. I didn't understand how we looked all that different. However, one day my husband came in to the tiny room we shared on the third floor, mad as he could be. When I noticed that he was taking off his shoes and grabbing the black shoe polish, I asked what had happened. He said that children were pointing to his brown and white saddle oxfords, jeering at him and throwing rocks at his shoes. As he painted the whole of each shoe with the black polish, I laughingly stated that he had advised me to ignore the taunts and maybe he should try to do that also.

"Jesus said, 'I leave you peace, my peace I give you, I do not give it to you as the world does. So don't let your hearts be troubled or afraid.'"

—*John 14:27*

We were living in Germany when the wall dividing East and West Germany was about to go up. Even before it went up, there was a big division in Berlin between the East and the West. People who got caught in the East behind the line who were not East Germans were often put in jail and had their cameras, money and other possessions confiscated. We had just read in the paper some of these horror stories when we were visiting in Berlin. One day when we were riding a train through parts of West Berlin, we missed the call to exit at the Brandenburg Gate before the train rolled on into East Germany. It became evident almost immediately that we had left West Berlin as the buildings became more bombed out, the people dressed shabbily and there was an ominous silence in the streets. There were hardly any moving cars. As the train rushed on down the tracks, we frantically pulled on the cords to stop the train. It was an action to no avail. The train stopped where it usually did. It was about one-half mile inside East Germany. In our broken German we tried to explain to the conductor that we needed to go back to the West and asked where we could get a train that returned us there. He told us where to go. We went to buy a ticket, but the ticket agent refused our money from West Germany and we had no U.S. dollars with us. There was only one solution. We would have to walk back the half mile, worrying constantly that we would be picked up as other people had been by the East German police. We faced the possibility of being thrown in jail and having our money and camera confiscated. The long blocks seemed endless. We were shaking violently! When we reached the wide street near the Brandenburg Gate where we would be safe once we reached the other side we started to run across. The East German policeman on the corner shouted, "Achtung!" at us. We froze in our tracks, certain that he was going to throw us in jail. Then he said in German, "Attention. Stop! You must use the crosswalk!" Never have two sets of legs covered a street crossing so fast.

Jane on a camel on one of her overseas trips.

Television Quiz Shows

o o o o o o o o o o o o o o o o o o o o o o o o o o o o o o o o o

"A gift is as a precious stone in the eyes of him that hath it; witherso-ever it turneth, it prospereth."

—*Proverbs 17:8*

One advantage of living in New Jersey during my early marriage is that we lived only about forty minutes from New York City. It was only a short ride on the train into the city. In order to earn a living for us so my husband could go to graduate school I took a job caring for children under the age of six. Six children plus my own three was the usual number who gathered at my home in Madison from 8:00 AM until 5:00 PM We had all sorts of playground equipment and early learning equipment from the best of stores. The children played store, house, heard stories and sang songs to the tunes to the children's records I had collected. At the same time I rented out a big house nearby, I furnished it with second hand furniture, and then I sublet it to five or six Bell Lab employees. I would take all the children with me to play in the rooms that I cleaned once a week. They thought the experience was a lark. On the weekend or holidays, when I was taking a vacation from the children, I would go into New York City on the train and go to the museums, the library and to Encore, a consignment shop where the television and movie stars took their clothes. The clothes were like new and the price was right.

Speaking of the "Price Is Right", my husband got to be on this show and on "Concentration." It was an exciting time for us when all the prizes started coming in. From that first show we received a whole set of Samsonite luggage. I forgot what we received from "Concentration" but when I was chosen for another game show I remember everything. I was given a red jump suit to wear that had a big band of magnetic tape on my backside so I could run about catching on the tape large feathers that were blown into the air. For every feather I caught, I was to answer a question and possibly get a prize.

An aunt later told me that she had just happened to be watching that same TV show and all she could see of me was my backside with large feathers coming toward the TV camera. I answered enough questions correctly to receive the following prizes: a year's supply of Sacony Knit clothes for my daughter and for me, a stove, a freezer, a Puritron, all kinds of camera equipment, a pedigree collie dog, tons of O'Cedar cleaning supplies and a year's supply of bread crumbs. I sold the stove and Puritron in order to pay taxes on the prizes. I sold the dog to someone who didn't mind it throwing up all the time as long as it had a pedigree. I gave the cleaning supplies and the boxes of bread crumbs to friends for house gifts. On the second round of questions they asked me, I would have won a diamond necklace, a fur coat and a trip to Europe had I answered any questions correctly. To this day, I know I answered the question correctly. The host of the show asked me the question, "What was Exodus?" I answered with great confidence, "Exodus is the second book of the Bible." Bong! Bong! The gong sounded that let the contestants and audience know that you had not answered the question correctly. "Sorry, that answer is wrong. The answer is 'a book by Leon Uris'." In my present life, my mature life, my confident life, I would protest their mistake until I proved that I had been correct. In those days, however, I was as meek as a sheep and accepted the loss.

When we went to California to visit my husband's family, we got on "Truth or Consequences" and won a vacuum cleaner. About this time when we were getting so confident that we would make our way through life getting on TV shows, the television executives came out with a new rule for people like us who were making the TV shows a hobby. The rule said that people who had previously been on TV game shows would have to wait seven years in order to participate in them again. Sadly, that rule ended this particular kind of fun. In those days before the new rules, I would sit in the TV audiences, study and figure out just who the people were who were selected and why they were selected. I came up with the idea that if one were tall, one could be seen when the audiences were asked to raise their hands, telling the host that he or she wanted to be on the show. Also it helped a lot to be blonde, assertive and Southern. The ones who picked the contestants seemed to like a deep Southern drawl, so being from the Deep South, in a foreign country (the North), I drawled to my best ability.

STARTING OVER

You, the sunshine,
Poured your warmth
Upon my dry cocoon body
Beckoning it to come forth.
The body which had long wrapped
Its dull folds
Around my spirit,
Somewhere down inside.
I could no longer
Stand the bonds,
The tightness of my confinement.
I burst the musty wrappings
Of the past,
Crawling carefully,
Slowly looking and perceiving all around me,
Before I spread my wings
And lept forth
With new found hope
Into the path of gliding winds.

Life Anew

"But those who marry will face many troubles in this life and I want to spare you this."

—I Corinthians 7:28

"Shall we indeed accept good from God and shall we not accept adversity."

—Job 3:10

After twenty-one years of marriage and nearly all the marriage counselors advising me to leave the marriage, I finally did just that. I did not believe in divorce but in this case there was no other answer. Near the end of the marriage my husband had asked me to get a real estate license in order to sell our mountain land. When he saw me thoroughly enjoying the real estate course and looking forward to my new goals outside the home, he announced, "It is either real estate or me!" I answered, "It is real estate!"

Now, as a single person, I tried to take on things that were overwhelming for me. Everything seemed to go wrong. My daughter had a horse and had no place to keep it when we left our large home to live in a small condo. An acquaintance from one of my classes said that she would keep the horse and feed it for a year without charging us in return for being able to ride it every day. After a year, the girl's new boyfriend called to say that he was getting ready to sell the horse as a payment for having kept and fed it for a year.

Since they broke our agreement, I rented a horse trailer and went out to the farm to reclaim our horse while the couple was at work. I roped the huge horse, Citation, formerly a racehorse. In order to get him into the trailer, I tied the rope around my fingers and fist, not realizing the potential problem. After a year of freedom running around the huge farm he did not want to enter the horse trailer. After roping him, I pulled hard. Citation reared back and the rope cut through my fingers like a cheese cutter on a block of cheese. Two of the fingers were cut off at the first knuckle. Because of the shock and horror, I don't think I felt the pain. I gathered up the two pieces of fingers in my jacket pocket and ran. The horse ran away. I headed toward the nearest farmhouse and fainted. The farmer's wife wrapped the fingers in a wet washcloth and then called the ambulance. I then called a professor friend from the University of Denver to come and find the horse and obtain the car that I had borrowed from him. The trailer was still attached and needed to be returned to the rental agency.

Since it took so long to reach the hospital from out in the country, one of the fingers was not in any condition to "take" after the surgeon sewed it back on. Thank God, the index finger "took" and healed. Because I now had only nine fingers, I couldn't play the organ, piano and guitar, all of which I had spent years learning. The accident also affected my ability to type. This happened just as I was trying to get up the speed of my typing in order to get a temporary secretarial job while I was learning the business of real estate. In the future when my fingernails were first manicured, I asked if I could get a discount for having only nine fingers. The manicurist shook her head and said, "A special problem always costs more!"

Since I had moved out of my home, I had no place to go. A fellow real estate salesman said that he would let me stay free in one of his empty rentals. He said he did not plan to rent it out until the following spring, as he had to do some redecorating. I bought kitchen supplies, a TV, new clothes, and food. Settling in, I took a long, deep breath hoping that I would at last have peace. I needed time to think about what I was going to do with the rest of my life. I needed time to pray.

A friend invited me to visit her in the mountains so I went up for the weekend. When I returned, I could not get into my apartment. I knocked on the door and a young girl came to the door. I asked what she was doing in my apartment. She said that it was her apartment and that of her boyfriend. Frantically I cried out, "Where are my things? Where are my clothes and TV and all that I just purchased?" The two people laughed and said they didn't know anything about my things. They slammed the door in my face. They had acted guilty and ruthless. I couldn't believe that another awful thing was happening to me. Again and again in those horrific days I called on God for extra help. I did not feel that He was listening for many months as horrors kept happening. However, I did not give up. I prayed, "God, I cannot handle these things by myself. Only you know what is going on and why. Now that I am alone and desperately poor and helpless, I pray that you will be my Father, my Husband and my Friend and Helper."

Earlier, I had asked my fellow salesman why he had leased the apartment to someone else when he had told me that I could use it for many months. He apologized saying that this couple was willing to pay more than he asked for the rent and as I had been living there free, he decided to let them in. He said he had called to tell me that they were moving into my apartment. He could not reach me during the weekend because I was in the mountains. He advised me to take them to small claims court, but in the end I just went on with my life and chalked up the incident to another learning experience. I was having more of those than I needed.

FLYING BUTTRESSES

Oh, God,
Within your church's classic walls
There are no chains to hold me back.
My soul leaps forth unfettered and free.
My hopes and resolutions spiral toward Thee,
Unencumbered by the little stumbling blocks of life;
A teenager's self assertion, a husband's criticism,
A fellow worker's cutting comment, a broken disposal,
Two overlapping appointments,
The incessant rhythmic barking of the dog next door,
A broken sewing machine needle, the last in the house.
These things daily puncture the upward and outward
Thrust of my soul as it reaches toward thee,
As it strives to send me into all the world
As a light into darkness.
Lord, I cannot go. The darkness is here.
I am bound by earth's increasing demands and problems
And yet as I am swallowed up in the majesty of man's
Offering of love to Thee in the glorious blending
Melodies of the choir,
In the golden brush strokes of the masters,
For a fleeting, but spectacular moment,
I know and remember that I am made in your image
And that all things are possible.

Driving My First Moving Van

○ ○

"He shall return no more to his house, neither shall his place know him anymore."

—Job 7:10

I was accustomed to getting calls from Mama to come and help her in some way or other. As I was the child who lived the closest to her in Florida, it was easy for me to drive up to see her. But before I moved to Florida, I lived in Denver so when she called for help, I had to fly quite a distance.

Getting off the plane in Orlando one afternoon after a long and tiring trip to Florida, I met Mama at the baggage department. I had come to Florida from snowy Colorado thinking I might enjoy a few days at the beach. As I reached for my two big bags, Mama put her arm up to stop me and said, "Honey, don't touch those. They are too heavy for you. You will need all your strength to move my furniture tomorrow!" I was astonished at her statement, since she not specifically told me why she wanted me to come to Florida to visit. I had planned to rest or go to the beach.

"Mama, what are you talking about? Do you really want me to move your furniture?"

She said, "Honey, I have just rented a moving van for you to drive to my new retirement home with my furniture. I got a call that the retirement home can get me in right away if I hurry up there in the next few days."

"Mama, I don't know how to drive a moving van!"

"Oh, Honey, the moving company man said it wouldn't be hard for you to drive it, and he would let you practice driving around the parking lot."

So this was my first introduction to driving moving vans and recreational vehicles. There were going to be at least ten more experiences to come in the next few years.

Mama had owned this particular home in Orlando only for a very short time. Her letter had described a darling home on a lake with a big oak tree. It sounded grand! When I arrived there with Mom in her yellow VW to the house, I noted a yellow stucco cottage that couldn't have been more than 1000 square feet. (Mama's favorite color was yellow.) The house was on a busy street and had a tiny pond in the back yard. There was an oak tree, as she had said, but my imagined picture of her dwelling faded somewhat as I peered at the house.

Mama had a habit of buying an inexpensive house, fixing it up for a song and then selling it and making a small profit. Her ability to decorate was so great that one almost didn't notice other failings in the house. One house she built did not have the necessary halls so one had to walk through another bedroom to get to a back bedroom. She said that her having to leave off halls from the architectural plans was not her fault. In one manse the church deacons had been unable to extend her as much money as had been promised to build so that she had to subtract something. She couldn't leave off a bedroom, so the halls went first.

Another unique thing that she did when building our family house on the golf course in Mobile, Alabama, was to add a slot in the dining room right behind the dining table where we could throw our paper plates into a can in the garage and never have to take them to the kitchen. After all, we didn't have a dishwasher.

Now, back to Mama's Orlando home, which she had only owned for about a year. We arrived from the airport and she let me go ahead of her through the house. I exclaimed with delight at the charming décor! The wood floors were covered with beautiful and colorful red and blue oriental rugs. Her primitive antiques lined the walls in glowing pine. The handmade Pennsylvania Dutch Casa was alive with bright colors. As I walked through the living room, I noted that Mama was down on the floor, crawling along behind me, rolling up the carpets as I walked over them. I said, "Mama, what are you doing?" I was astonished!

"Honey, you have seen everything now! It is time to pack and get on our way!"

"Here is your bedroom," she said as we walked into a small front bedroom. I sat down wearily on the red and white quilt, which was draped across the antique cannonball bed. Standing in the door with her hands on her hips, she screamed with horror as I collapsed on the bed. "Oh, no," she screamed. "You will break the three hundred year-old stitches in my antique quilt." With one sweep of her arm, she moved me off the bed and began rolling up the quilt into a tidy bundle, which she carefully placed on the chest of drawers. Then she bent down and rolled up the bedroom carpets. After that she went after the pictures on the wall and piled them on top of a blanket chest. She reminded me again that I had now seen everything anyway. By now the room looked quite barren. I had not had much time to enjoy the bright colors of the décor before it was all gone, rolled up and plopped in against the corner wall. "After all," she stated, "we have to load all this stuff into the van and be at the retirement home by afternoon tomorrow."

Wearily, I grabbed my robe and went into the bathroom, which she had pointed out on my way through the house. There was a bathtub surrounded by several racks of lovely pink washcloths and towels, which were sewn with satin baskets of flowers and satin edging. After running the hot water, undressing and climbing into the tub, I was lying back relaxing while Mama continued to work on the house around me. Scrubbing my face after the long, dirty trip on the plane, I was suddenly shocked into reality when Mama flung open the door and screamed, "Oh, no, did you use my beautiful pink linen washrag? Those are just for looks! Here, give me those," and she flung herself into the room, grabbing the untouched towels as well as the washcloth that I was using. Sweeping out of the room and returning hastily, she threw me a well-worn and ragged washcloth and told me to use that instead.

Little by little Mama and I loaded the van with most of the light furnishings, boxes and rugs. She paid a couple of neighborhood boys to carry the heavy furniture. Mama had a way with youth and children as she showed an interest in them personally and told them fascinating stories from life and the Bible. She never missed a chance to witness to her Lord. God was more important to her than anything else, but second to Him was her family and third was decorating. She never spent much money on her antiques. She could find a bargain anywhere. When she started collecting in the 1930s, antiques were not as popular as in today's world. Daddy would give her the $5.00 fee from a wedding he had conducted, and with the money she would find an antique.

In the mountains of West Virginia where my Daddy had his first church, she would go out into the back roads and if she saw an antique sitting on a cabin porch, she would go up to the owner and promise to give them $5.00 or to trade a piece of Sears and Roebuck furniture for the chest. Most of the mountain people preferred new furniture to old furniture and the antiques were just junk to them. They were glad to trade.

Over the years Mama built up quite a large amount of antique furniture, which rarely cost her much money. Preachers' families didn't have much to spend in those days. She gave away a lot of the furniture to her children and there was still enough to fill a rented moving truck to the top of its ceiling.

The next day, we were on the road by noon. Mama was driving the small yellow VW Bug, loaded with colorful shoes and dresses thrown loosely on the back seat of the car. She didn't bother to pack them as we only had a three-hour drive she said. Boxes and suitcases take up extra room. There were not going to be any neighbor boys to help us unpack at the other end. I wondered what her plan for that would be. I shouldn't have worried. There was a handful of elderly gentlemen waiting at the other end. I wondered how they knew she was coming! They must have met her when she was registered to live Penny Farms.

Meanwhile, during the three hour drive north on I-95, Mama tooted along in the little old Bug while I nervously tried to handle the big steering wheel and shift the worn gears of the 15 foot moving van. She was moving along fast as if she were eager to see the folks at this retirement center where she had reserved one efficiency room for all her furniture and clothes and one small separate room for her organ. I really had not learned to drive the van in the parking lot of the rental place. No one offered to teach me how to drive. At the Ryder Rental Store, I had just turned on the engine and drove where there was space, trying not to hit the other parked cars. Now I was on a highway where each car was trying to beat out the car in front or in back of them. Truckers were delighted to honk at me. I guess I was going too slowly for them although I felt like I was speeding, trying to keep up with Mama.

We had only gone about 45 minutes out of Orlando when suddenly Mama was honking her horn and waving wildly from the window. She was pointing toward the fields on her left and beyond. Not knowing what she wanted I gradually pulled the big van over to the side, out of the way of traffic. She stopped the VW also. Carefully I climbed down from the high truck, walked to her car and asked, "What is going on? What's wrong?"

"Oh, Honey, I was just telling you that I use to live about twenty miles in that direction. You didn't have to stop!"

Jane ready to drive her first Ryder truck.

WINTER IN COLORADO

A skier pushes off from the over-arching crest
Of the cliff and drops into the soft depths
Of the unseen hill below,
Taking with him traces of past tracks,
Plunging into the heart of shifting powder snow,
Shivering with excitement
At the day's blue and white crispness,
The wonder of being alone above the world
In God's fantastic creation.
He races forward, feeling the body of earth
Heave and swell,
Feeling that all worldly ills are washed clean,
Renewed, thrown in the air behind.
No one can catch him.
Power, beauty and understanding are his.
Suddenly he leaves behind the overwhelming hugeness
Of the universe he feels on the mountaintop.
Now he descends into the forest below.
Trees surround him on every side.
The black and silent woods rise above him,
And seem to move slowly in on him
With a gentle protectiveness.
His movements are now muffled in a featherbed of snow.
He slows to a halt and stands quietly,
Almost without breathing for a moment,
Listening to the pure stillness of the forest.
He has enjoyed the wild excitement and climatic moments
Of skiing.
He has flung his body into every known contortion
As he flies upon his skis,

Breathing deeply of the thrills and passions of this sport.
But this stillness, this reflecting, this isolation
Is also a part of skiing,
And for the moment, it is enough.

STUCK UNDER SNOW

Once long ago in Denver
When stuck beneath the snow
When under mountain avalanche
At fifty or below,

I dreamed I saw a lot of white
And it appeared quite warm.
I burrowed underneath its folds
Which kept me from death's harm.

I dreamed that if I lived to tell
About that nightmare cold,
I'd move to where the white was warm,
And in the sand, grow old.

I went to sunny Florida
To live a simple style,
I traded winter weather
For stalled cars in a pile.

I learned to travel the back streets
And shop on rainy days
But then, the shopping strips became
An endless busy maze.

I still admire the warmth and sun
The lazy floating lakes
The towering oaks and happy birds,
The fun that Disney makes.

I'm glad I went where snow can't go
Where beaches are profuse,
But I'm hoping to live to see
A monorail in use!

Double Trouble

"I sought the Lord, and he answered me: he delivered me from all my fears."

—Psalm 34:24

"A certain Samaritan, as he journeyed, came upon him; and when he saw him, he felt compassion."

—Luke 10:33

After my marriage was over, I continued to live and work in Denver selling real estate for six years. One spring in Denver I was dressed in toeless high heels and a beige summer cotton suit. I had left the flat plains of Denver to go up into the mountains near Winter Park Ski area to list a group of condominiums. As the car climbed higher and higher in the mountains, the snow started and began to come down in an almost blinding fashion. These spring storms could come unexpectedly and quickly. In my rush to leave for the mountains, I forgot to bring warmer clothes and blankets. I did remember to bring my two big dogs, a Lab and a Husky. They accompanied me wherever I went. As I neared Boreas Pass, the snow became heavier and wetter! Before I knew it, my car slid off the road and down a six-foot embankment. The dogs and I had hit the steering wheel and the dashboard but were not injured. At first I was confident that someone would notice the skid marks, stop and help me. I climbed out of the car but found it impossible to walk up the hill in the toeless heels. The cold and the wind were causing me to shiver uncontrollably. Back at the car I tried to run the heater, but after some hours the gas ran out. I reached into the back trunk and got out the real estate sign that I had planned to put up when I listed the condominium complex. I stuck it in the snow on top of the car and tried to attract attention.

Several cars stopped, and their drivers promised to call for help. The help never came. I tried to stay warm by huddling between the dogs. That action helped somewhat. Hours went by and my hopes were about gone as the cars on the pass dwindled to only a few passing by. The snow fell harder and my tracks were long gone. As usual in most of my daily experiences, I spent a great deal of my time praying. I said to God if He would send help and if I could get out alive then I would immediately move to a place where the "white stuff" was warm instead of cold. Florida was on my mind. Hot sand and beaches were on my mind. I have found that God always has unusual ways of making us sit up and take notice when He wants us to move on. This might have been one of those times. I would never have left Colorado if this incident had not happened. I adored everything about the state. God must have had other plans for me and I was to find out about them later.

> *"I waited patiently for the Lord; and He inclined to me, and heard my cry. He also brought me out of a horrific pit."*
>
> *—Psalm 40:1*

I had been stranded for ten hours. About 2:00 AM I heard the sound of a motor coming up the road. The car stopped and the driver peered over the side and asked if I needed help. After conversation with his three friends and some maneuvering, he was able to get the steel cable from his van's wench to reach down to me and pull my car out of the ditch. Then they gave me enough gas to get to the next station. I believe I heard them say that they were dentists on a ski trip and they had heard about the car off the road at the last filling station. In my mind they were angels sent by God to rescue me.

The next day after arriving at my vacation home in Dillon, I called the owner of the condo that I was supposed to list and explained the reason I had not shown up. Then, after catching up on sleep and warming my frozen bones for a few extra hours, I called Ryder and rented their two largest trucks. I decided to go to the "Land of Sand": Florida. There were relatives in Orlando and my Mom had grown up there and in Deland so it seemed to be the logical place to go. It would take two vans for all the stuff I had in the Denver home and in the one in Dillon. I didn't worry about selling the home or leaving my job. I figured like Scarlett, I could worry about it tomorrow. It had been six years since my divorce. My doctor brother had co-signed for me to get a loan and I had done well in real estate and I had hung out at many garage sales.

My present job was to find someone to drive one of the moving vans and I would drive the other one. I had "learned" to drive a van in a parking lot when I went to Florida once on vacation to help my Mama. Suddenly I realized that I knew the perfect solution. My son Rob was on his Spring Break from the University of Colorado at Boulder. I called him and in no time at all he agreed to help me. I promised him that he would be well paid, as any other driver would be paid.

I picked up one Ryder truck in the mountains near Dillon, hired some men to load it and headed for Denver the next day. The roads on the side of the mountains near Loveland Pass warned me about the possibility of the truck's running away on the steep mountain roads. Area after area along the road had runaway ramps where the trucks that had lost their brakes could be slowed down. These signs and ramps added to my frustration and fears. However, I was too excited over the big trip ahead to let it bother me for very long. I proceeded carefully down the road toward Denver where I was to meet my son and pick up another Ryder truck.

To make a long story short, after meeting Rob and having hired men and Rob load the second van we took off on our way to Florida (a five day trip) going only fifty miles an hour thanks to Ryder speed governors. Rob was in the lead. I could not stand to be away from the dogs, so they rode with me. Just before leaving Denver, I had purchased a pair of walkie-talkies so that the two of us could communicate as we drove. I drove with my two large dogs. I also pulled my small thirteen-foot Boler camping trailer behind my van. The trailer was where we four would all sleep at night.

Rob and dog Cope before leaving Colorado for Florida.

"You were wearied by all your ways, but you would not say, 'it is hopeless.'
You found renewal of your strength and so you did not faint."

—Isaiah 57:10

The trip was slow and tedious. When we first started, I would call Rob on the walkie-talkie and announce that we needed to stop for a bathroom break. Rob decided that we shouldn't make such private talk over the air and should have a code word that we used as we drove. The code words were "Tasha" and "Cope", named for the two dogs. We realized before long that plan would not work. "Tasha" and "Cope" were very restless on the long trip and kept pacing up and down my wide van seat. They would rarely go to sleep and when they did sleep, I was eager for them to stay that way for a good while. So when Rob's voice boomed over the airways, calling out "Tasha" and "Cope" they would jump up from a deep sleep and pace again. We changed the code words.

Early one night near Houston, we pulled up to sleep in the suburbs of a town near a high school. The neighborhood looked rather safe and quiet. We let the dogs out to go to the bathroom and they ran away. I was terrified that they wouldn't find their way back. For some minutes my heart beat like a drum as I pictured them lost forever. But, they returned at long last. Once they returned, we finally settled into the trailer for the night. I slept on the bed while Rob slept on the five foot wide sofa and the dogs slept on the floor. Rob who was six feet four inches tall had to prop his feet on the sink's counter by the side of the small sofa. We were so tired that we fell sound asleep quickly. Suddenly a marching band awakened us. What a surprise at that time of night! We peered out the windows and saw all the lights blazing in a room at the back of the school where the band must have gathered for a late night practice. One musical production followed another until we finally had to dress and move the vans to another spot. This time we found another place but when the firecrackers started exploding near where we were sleeping we decided we would just stay and ignore them.

Numerous unusual experiences happened during those five days on the road, but a unique experience happened after crossing the Florida line. There was a Truck Weight Station near the Florida line. Neither Rob nor I were sure if we were to stop. We felt we were driving trucks but the big truckers didn't consider us in their same category. We didn't stop. A bit further down the highway I noticed that a Highway Patrolman was coming up rapidly behind us. I called Rob on the walkie-talkie and asked if he knew anything we might have done wrong. He answered that he had some traffic tickets from Boulder that he had not as yet paid. By then, the patrolman was pulling up behind Rob's moving van and wedging his patrol car between the two of us. I watched as the two men spoke and then walked to the back of Rob's van. As Rob pushed up the big van door on the back of the van, all kinds of shoes, plastic dishes, loose boxes and bags rained down on the Highway Patrolman's head as well as that of Rob. In Denver when we were at the last part of the packing of the vans, we had run out of places for the boxes to be piled. So we had thrown separate articles into any crack or space we could find in the back of our trucks. The movement during the trip had loosened the extra stuff and the opening of the door had dislodged it on the top of the heads of these two men. I found out later that the patrolman was looking for plants that we might have brought across the state line. We had none.

The scene in front of me was like a Charlie Chaplin movie. I watched the patrolman duck and grab his hat to protect it when the stuff started falling. Then the two men picked up numerous articles, replaced them and slammed the door of Rob's van. I couldn't help but laugh! But then I saw them headed toward the back of my van. Now it wasn't funny! I jumped down from the high seat and followed them. When we arrived in the back of the van the patrolman was getting ready to look for plants when a huge tractor-trailer passed us on the highway. As it passed, it sucked the big brown, wide brimmed hat of the Highway Patrolman and also pulled off my wig and blew them across the field. (It's convenient to wear a wig when traveling rather than stopping at a beauty shop and getting one's hair done along the way. Underneath the wig my hair was platted in multiple little braids that stuck straight out from my head.) The Highway Patrolman was by now galloping across the field to retrieve whatever blew off. He picked up his hat and my wig and came running back. And as he plopped my wig on my head, he put it on backwards so I couldn't see. He put his large brown wide brimmed hat on his head next. After turning the wig around so I could see, I asked, "Would you like to look into my van also?" As he ran toward his car, he shouted over the sound of the traffic, "LADY, I'VE SEEN ENOUGH!" He jumped into his police car and took off down the road as if he had seen a ghost!

FLORIDA TRAFFIC

Jangled nerves and Type-A hearts
Frenzied waits…with stops and starts—
Foolish persons' weaving feats,
Broken mains and torn-up streets.
Fenders deep in flooded roads,
Squashed raccoons and smashed green toads,
Leaving late then blocked by trains,
Side road stops, deluging rains.
Up above, the clouds float by
While down below, we fret and sigh!
The only thing that keeps us sane,
Is hope that there's a right turn lane!

HOMES

Homes vary greatly
Some showy and fine,
Dignified, modest
Artistic or pine
Japanese walls
Spanish tile floors,
Triangular, mobile
Heavy wood doors
But mine is special
Inviting and warm,
Jovial, handsome
A cove from the storm!
Whatever it has,
It needs to suit me,
No other should state
What it has to be!

The Kitchen Story

One morning some years after I had moved Mama to her retirement home, I received a call from her. She sounded quite frantic and in need of help. "Honey, could you run up here and help me sell my cabin? You are in real estate and would know why it will not sell, even though everyone says it is the cutest place they have ever seen." She had built a log cabin on a beautiful little river near Jacksonville where she and Clarence could go for breaks from the retirement home some twenty miles away. She had only had the cabin a short time when she was ready to sell it because her health as well as that of Clarence had deteriorated substantially.

I jumped in the car and drove the three hours to her beautiful little spot on the river. As I walked from room to room, I was intrigued with her décor and charm in the cabin. I went through the living room, the bathroom, the family room and her bedroom. There were no halls. It was a small cabin but something big was missing. "Honey," she questioned me again, "Why won't it sell? Maybe you can help me?"

"Mama," I said, "it doesn't have a kitchen! Most people want kitchens!"

She looked absolutely shocked. "I don't understand why that's a problem." She pulled the checkered red sofa away from the wall in the family room and said, "Look here. I left this hole behind the sofa in case anyone wanted to put a stovepipe through here and make a kitchen over here on the table and have a hot plate. Also, you can eat over at the 'Pick and Save' and that way no one will gain excessive weight. I tell everyone that but they just shake their heads and move on."

"Mama," I said, "most people can't even imagine what a house or room would look like when it's painted a different color. They certainly aren't going to be able

114

to imagine a kitchen in place in this family room. You are just going to have to have a carpenter build a kitchen in here if you are going to sell it." She looked devastated!

After a short visit, I returned to Orlando to my home and a week later received a call from Mama. The sound in her voice assured me that she had a smile on her face. "Guess what, Honey. The carpenter added a counter, cabinet, sink, stove and refrigerator in the family room. I sold the house to the first people who came in the door."

We had started out with normal kitchens during my early childhood but after Mama found that she had a tendency to gain weight easily, she figured if there was no kitchen she might not eat as much. However, there were others in the family and life must go on. We all liked food. I mostly remember eating cheese or mayonnaise sandwiches at home but we were invited out a lot to homes of members of the congregation. After Mama started designing and building her own homes, the kitchen spaces got smaller and smaller until they were entirely gone. One owner of one of Mama's former houses showed me a large closet where she said Mama's former kitchen stood. Believe me, I remembered it well. Its size didn't inspire "Creative Cooking."

Real Estate: The Prayer

"For if I pray in an unknown tongue, my spirit prayeth, but my understanding is unfruitful."

—*I Corinthians 14:13*

Our real estate office in Orlando was quite a large one. It was made up of all types of people, both men and women. It was rather an unusual office in that the manager always had an opening prayer before the weekly office meeting. Different Realtors were invited to have the prayer. I was called on more than once because I was known as a PK which means "Preacher's Kid." Also, I was an elder at my church. This particular week, my boss told me a few days ahead that I should be prepared to have the opening prayer on that next Tuesday morning. It just so happened that I had been part of a conference at the church that chose to study the life of Mother Teresa and her emphasis on giving of yourself and service rather than going for individual success in life.

Rather than just making up a prayer that Tuesday morning, I had worked very hard to write a prayer on a 5 by 7 card which emphasized Self Sacrifice in a person rather than Success. The meeting was called together and all sixty salesmen became quiet as my boss announced, "Jane will now open our meeting with prayer."

I stood up and said, "Let us bow our heads." After the group shut their eyes, I pulled out my 5 by 7 card and began to read. "Dear Lord, we as Realtors have a burning desire for...Sex!" Of course, I had stumbled over the word "success" and the unintended and shocking word that came out was "sex." The place echoed with gasps and screams of laughter. I had worked so long and hard on the prayer that I didn't want it to be wasted so I started the prayer again. "Let us bow our heads..." I was not able to finish. The meeting was a disaster for our Broker as it was punctuated with laughter on and off for the rest of the hour.

After the meeting was finished, individuals often ran to the phone to get messages right before leaving on the large Greyhound-size bus that took the salesmen to see all the new listings for that week. I was late in getting on the bus. When I climbed aboard, I noted that the women were all sitting in the front of the bus. In the rear of the bus, each man was saving an empty seat next to himself and beckoning to me to come and share his seat.

Speaking of prayer, there were many times when I would ask for Mama's advice on a certain subject such as marriage, divorce and poverty. Mama was thrifty in everything except prayer. One particular day I called from Denver to ask for her advice again. She launched into complete detail about my problem, asking for God's direction. The prayer went on for about ten minutes. When she finished I said, "Mama, I thank you for your prayer and so does AT&T."

REAL ESTATE

You've chosen me to list your house
To market and to sell…
The confidence you've shown me
You've done it all so well.

My job is now to keep in touch
To let the public know
That your place has great amenities
That I am proud to show.

Real Estate: Sale of the Dwarf's Home

○ ○
"In all the work you are doing, work the best you can—work as if you were doing it for the Lord, not for people."

—*Colossians 3:23*

When a home is to be sold, the listing agent who is chosen to sell the home must take a careful look at all aspects of the home and then advise the owners as to what needs to be done in order to make a good and expedient sale. When I first arrived at a home in Orlando to meet the owners of a possible new listing, I was pleased to notice the elevation of the home, the big old oak trees and the lovely pool. However, what hit me from the moment I climbed out of my automobile was the abundance of multicolored, stone gnomes and dwarfs in the front yard. Some were pushing wheelbarrows and turning cartwheels. Others were standing on their heads and some were lying under stone toadstools. There were also a wide variety of whirly gigs scattered around the yard. I could hardly see the house for the myriad of characters and objects in the yard. My thoughts were in a jumble as to what I would say to the owners about the need to remove these items. I never liked to hurt anyone's feelings for obviously the owners were delighted with their chosen décor.

Inside the home, the owners proudly showed me numerous rooms of average size. Not a thing seemed to be wrong with the size or color. However, dancing on every surface of every table or chest were many varieties of clowns, in every position known to man. Some were made of wood; some cloth, some wire but most were bright colored ceramics. On the walls, instead of seascapes and landscapes in frames, there were hundreds of dancing, vaulting, twirling clowns.

Knowing that there would be little chance of selling this house as it was, I silently prayed for the right answer for these dear people who were so obviously glad to show off their home. After 15 years in real estate, I knew the strong feelings about one's own choice of home and design. Mr. Johnson said that he felt their home should bring in more money than similar homes on their street. I stated, "Mr. Johnson, may I ask why you feel that your home should bring in more than houses similar to yours?"

Mr. Johnson glanced proudly at his beaming wife who already was nodding her home in agreement even before he said any words at all. "My Honey here can decorate anything! She really has a touch when it comes to color, texture, and movement. Plus we have our lifelong collections that are eye catchers for the house. It makes a nice experience for everyone."

I answered, "Mr. Johnson, are you planning to include the decorations on the lawn and the clowns in the price of what you are asking for the house?"

"Mercy no," he responded, startled by my suggestion, "not our collections. We have a fortune in all those figurines. We just want to sell the house!"

Suddenly I was provided with an idea! "Mr. and Mrs. Johnson, you certainly have a lovely home and pool that should be marketable. However, I am very concerned about one thing. I am afraid that when possible buyers come to see the house, they will see only your great variety of collections." True! "They may not even be very aware of what the house looks like as they will be so busy looking at your collections. Knowing how real estate works, often buyers will say, 'I will pay the price that you are asking, but you must throw in the washer and dryer, and some of the furniture for the same price.' Now in your case, they may ask for your lifelong collections which you say are worth thousands of dollars to be thrown in free of charge. I have no idea if that would really happen, but it is possible. I have seen it happen in many cases over the years. However, to be on the safe side, in order to preserve your collections and also to protect them from carelessly being bumped or broken, I would rent a temporary storage unit for just a month and move all the clowns and gnomes into the storage where they will be safe until the house sells."

Mrs. Johnson was elated with the idea. The next time I returned to check on the house and its status for putting it on the market, the collections had been cleared out and the home looked refreshingly like any other ranch house with a pool that was for sale in the surrounding neighborhoods. "Thank you, thank you," Mrs. Johnson said. "Thank you for saving our valuable collections. That was such a good idea about obtaining a storage unit."

The house sold within two weeks!

MY HOME

Oh home, my home…
What welcome arms
Reach out and call me back.
My heart leaps forth
When first I see
Its door and chimney stack.

The mouse may have his castle
King Kong, his hidden cave
But when I leave my work at night,
This home I'll always crave!

Sale of My Home

o o o o o o o o o o o o o o o o o o o o o o o o o o o o o o o o
"We…have joy with our troubles, because we know that these troubles produce patience. And patience produces character and character produces hope."

—*Romans 5:3–4*

During my real estate days in Orlando, I lived in one of the lovely older areas of town with huge oaks, several lakes and beautiful homes. However, it was near a real old part of town where the mall was closing down and people were moving to newer homes and more modern shopping centers. The sales of houses in my area were moving slowly. You might say that the bubble had burst in that housing market. However, I needed to sell and go to a less expensive home as I had spent too much of my time playing tennis and golf and had neglected my real estate business. So I put up a large company sign with my name on it as the Listing Agent, "List with Frist." My other signs said, "Insist on Frist."

My highest boss in our real estate company, Merrill Lynch, lived in the neighborhood also. He jogged by my home every morning. One day he jogged right up to my front door and rang the bell. When I came to the door he queried, "When are you going to sell this house? It's embarrassing to have our company sign sitting there for so long!"

I answered, "Now, Rob, you and I both know that this neighborhood is going down even though it is a gorgeous area. It is not my fault. It is the fault of the neighborhood!"

He looked up at the ceiling of the porch and pointed out there were cobwebs way up there in the corner. "See," he said, "that is why the house hasn't sold. Go get me a broom and I will fix it!"

After I retrieved the broom from the far recesses of the home, he took it and slapped away at the ceiling, sweeping and knocking down any webs or bugs that were there. That was the first time I had looked up at the ceiling in two years.

After all I had come from Colorado where bugs and spiders weren't on the porch ceilings. "Now," he said, with a certain amount of pride and satisfaction, "your house will sell right away and I want you to give me 3% of the commission when it does."

"Oh, sure, sure!" I knew that his cleaning off of the webs on the ceiling wouldn't make a bit of difference to the sale of the home. Do you know what happened within a week? I sold the home. Did I give my boss a commission? Ask me some other time. That is another story!

Southern Manners

This story is about one of my listings that I shall never forget. The house that I had listed was a plain and ordinary one. It took quite a while to sell. It was a buyer's market and people were not buying this one. Meanwhile, Mr. Lee, the seller, got restless and decided to leave the house and to move across town. But summertime in Denver is when the grass is watered a lot and grows fast. The head of the house returned weekly to mow the lawn at his now empty house. One afternoon when I was showing the house, I drove Mrs. Livingstone, a possible buyer, to preview the house before her husband saw it.

We moved quickly through the empty rooms in the front part of the house, and when we reached the back bathroom, I shoved the door open and was immediately horrified to see Mr. Lee sitting on the john with his slacks dropped to the floor. Everything above the lowered slacks was showing in plain view. Though I was shocked, my Southern training went into automatic action. My social graces took over. I blurted, "Mr. Lee, meet Mrs. Livingstone." Mrs. Livingstone leaned forward, stuck out her hand to shake his. He abruptly stood up, trying to pull up his pants with one hand while shaking her outstretched hand with his other hand. She weakly responded with propriety and thoughtfulness. "Please don't get up, Mr. Lee."

The moment was so embarrassing for all of us that Mrs. Livingstone turned and quickly fled back through the house with me on her heels. When we were outside, after catching our breath, we nearly doubled over with screams of laughter. Needless to say, after this episode, I communicated only with Mr. Lee's wife by phone until I at last sold the house.

Broken Bones

"Jesus said, 'These things I have spoken to you that in Me you may have peace. In the world you will have tribulation, but be of good cheer. I have overcome the world."

—*John 16:33*

The week that I fell and broke two different extremities on two different days was the first time I realized that I had osteoporosis. The first broken bones happened when I was taking food to an old man living next door. He gallantly escorted me down the front stairs of his home, but as he had large proportions, his body took up most of the width of the stairs as we descended. Unfortunately I fell off the stairs sideways and broke the anklebones in my left foot. After an emergency visit to the hospital, this same neighbor returned the favor and brought food to me. After a few days of not exercising because of the cast, I began to gain weight. I bought yogurt and grapes for nourishment. While walking on my new crutches, I slipped on one of the grapes and fell on the living room floor. The pain in my right arm was so bad that I realized I probably had another broken bone or two. Unable to rise from the floor, I pulled the phone cord with my teeth and the phone fell on the floor where I was able to make an emergency call to my daughter, Jane Alden, who lived in the same town. "Oh, no, not again. I am just leaving for the airport and can't help you but I will call a friend to take you to the hospital." Jane Alden's male friend was less than happy to be a good Samaritan on this day, but after dropping me in the Emergency Room, he made the rounds finding cute nurses and ended up leaving the hospital with a new young nurse girlfriend, leaving me with no way to get home.

For the next six weeks, I was unable to fully dress myself in order to get to work at my real estate office. Buttons, hooks and earrings were especially impossible to maneuver so I would throw on a robe over my pajamas and put a bedroom slipper on the driving foot, throw my clothes and makeup in a bag and drive to the office for much needed help in getting dressed. I refused to stop working and continued to hobble on crutches behind possible buyers as the looked at houses, sometimes five at a time. No one expressed their thoughts, but I feel sure that they were less than thrilled with their slow, crippled salesman.

Just as I was preparing to submit this book to the publisher, I fell over a board by an exercise machine where I exercised daily. I broke the large femur bone in my right leg. I was admitted to the Emergency Room at the hospital. I was released to go home after receiving an x-ray, a cast and a pair of crutches. Walking on crutches takes some ability and I had forgotten how to do it. I fell again late at night trying to hop to the bathroom. Falling two times in the next two nights, I made the break worse and lay on the tile floor all night, unable to attract help from my screams of pain. Mary, my high school roommate had allowed me to stay in the street-level apartment of her huge home while I had a broken leg. My own home had twenty steps down to its entrance but Mary's home was so well insulated that she couldn't hear my screams when I fell two more times. She found me asleep on the floor in the morning.

The next day I was taken back to the doctor and a new x-ray revealed that I had broken the leg even further and that I would need an operation to put pins in my leg. After several days at the hospital, I was sent to a well-known Rehabilitation Center in our area. Above my bed and on the wheelchair were placed two red signs warning the nurses that I must always be accompanied everywhere as I was at high risk for further falls. Because I was accustomed to doing everything by myself for so many years, it was rather difficult for me to wait patiently for a nurse after ringing for help. Once when the nurse took too long to come, I went to the bathroom on the walker unaccompanied. As a result, the frightened and angry nurse put me back in bed, turned on the emergency light on my bed so it would flash a brilliant red should I ever move an inch from the bed again. I heard later that because of my eagerness to keep moving, to learn the physical therapy and to work on my book, the administrator of the hospital put the following words in my file: "Motivated but impulsive!"

This experience was not in vain, for during the three months of healing, my soul was healed from all the many visits, calls, cards, flowers and showers of food I received from a very caring and generous community. My son, Rob, who lives close by ran hundreds of errands during the three months of recovery and visited me two or three times a day. My daughter, Jane Alden, who had her certification in shiatsu from Hawaii, gave me numerous massages to help the pain. Good Samaritans abound in my life and for that I am forever grateful.

Rob, Jane Alden and David all grown up.

TO A FRIEND

Just a note to say
Your friendship touched me
In a special way.
I reached out for your friendship,
You reached out toward my pain,
This meant more to me than words can say.
In a world where much is cold
Too far apart,
Afraid of truth,
Your honesty and goodness to me
Told me that part of life's meaning
Is in scenes such as we shared.
I've often asked God,
"Why me?
Why this?"
And never been given an answer.
But yesterday in a small way,
He answered me and said,
"Your struggles were given to you
In order that you might share
Your hours of pain
With others who also for a moment
Have lost their way
And wandered frightened
In the same forest
Of pain and questioning
That you, too, have entered.

Difficult Times

○ ○

"Therefore is my spirit overwhelmed within me; my heart within me is desolate."

—Psalm 143:4

When I first moved to Orlando the house I had bought with borrowed money, was about to go into foreclosure as I wasn't making much money at all. I was also flying back to Colorado for court dates concerning the divorce. At that same time, the IRS was including me in its yearly audit. On top of this, my two big dogs, the Husky and the Lab, opened the sliding glass door to my patio, ran out and chased a woman on a bike. One of the dogs grabbed her foot and bit it. This was the dog who had been abused as a pup by a bicyclist who had thrown rocks and cans at him when riding down the alley where he was staying.

My insurance company was sued for $78,000 because the lady who was bitten missed work for two weeks as a broker of commodities and also endured pain and suffering. The dogs had to be put to sleep. I was so inconsolable that even my minister called on me to give me comfort. The next time I got dogs, the insurance company told me they needed to be small ones. Thus, poodles came into my life.

God has always been my present helper in my life, but in these difficult days He and I spent a lot of time in discussion. Mama had always talked about the power of Satan in our lives. After these experiences, I was sure that she was right about his presence on the earth as I had experienced him first hand. She had taught me that the closer one comes to God, the more that Satan attacks. Evil was trying to peck away at me everyday and I sank lower and lower in a pit of anguish, only to remember my faith and pull myself up a tiny bit, day after day. Eventually, I turned my life over totally to God, promising Him that I would no longer let fear overtake me as I had in the past. I never knew where the next penny was coming from. In order to pay bills I had to pull the shade down on my fears and just trust. Amazingly, I was never completely without money again. My hard work, getting up at 6:00 AM and going to the office and working until 9:00 at night paid off. I felt that God brought me the clients and gave me an insight into their needs and desires. At last I was able to see the light at the end of the tunnel.

THE STONE CATHEDRAL

Dear God
One Sunday I came tormented and torn
Into this tall stone cathedral.
I slipped into a pew which contained worn cushions
Of round and uneven lumps.
Those lumps gave discomfort during the service
To remind me of the sharp, cutting rocks
That life had scattered in my path this week.
I tried to look above the gravel of our lives
Into the ever changing blues and golds
Of the glowing stained glass windows before me.
I sat there thinking, "I am a stained saint in a glass window!"
Then the choir from above sang
And changed the dark moods of my soul with a warm and lifting
    melody.
Their song entered where no human feet dared to go.
Sweet music flowed forth and filled me with its message.
All of my weariness fell away and
And I was thankful for God's gift of music to the choir.
Lord God, I thank you.
May this choir offer their voices in song again today,
Placing their music like a dear hand upon the stiff hearts of your
    people.

Serving Communion

o o o o o o o o o o o o o o o o o o o o o o o o o o o o o o o o o

"Yet man is born unto trouble as the sparks fly upward."

—*Job 5:7*

Christmas was nearing. While shopping for Christmas gifts one day, I found a lovely red wool suit on sale. I was eager to try it out. Sunday was the following day so I wore it to church. At the last minute before the communion service, more elders were needed to distribute the elements among the congregation and I was asked to help.

The church was one of the largest congregations in the South and this particular Sunday was right before Christmas. I had passed down the aisles about half way, perhaps past twelve rows, when I noticed for the first time an unusual flapping sound behind and under my arm. I had not heard it before because the music of the organ had filled the auditorium. Now the organ's music came to a standstill. The flapping sound was persistent. Suddenly one woman from the pew shyly pointed to my sleeve, smiled and whispered, "Your store tags are still on your sleeve!"

There was nothing I could do but finish taking part in the service. My face was as red as the suit, and also hotter than the suit. When I reached the car after church, I pulled off the jacked and looked at the guilty tags. There were not only two tags stating the name of the store and the maker of the suit but there were tags saying "Sale Price" and there was a big bunch of numbers saying what I had paid for the suit. Included with this group of tags was a clear plastic envelope bearing gold buttons and a gold safety pin. I was never able to go back to distributing communion at that church again and it was not because of a lack of invitations. The congregation and the minister were very forgiving. However, my psyche had suffered a blow that I was unable to overcome.

Predestined to Move

○ ○

"By faith Abraham, when called to go to a place he would later receive as his inheritance, obeyed and went, even though he did not know where he was going."

—Hebrews 11:8

The largest moving company in Orlando sent a man to my house after I called and inquired of prices. He now snapped his clip board over the paper with the collected facts, finished climbing over moving boxes and furniture and then exclaimed, "Lady, it will cost you approximately $6,000 to move your possessions to North Carolina." He seemed worn out from the effort it had taken him to come to this ultimate conclusion. I felt sorry for him, but at that moment, I decided to move the possessions myself. The price for driving a rented moving van could not possibly be so high, I thought to myself. After the poor little man left, I picked up the phone and ordered a thirty-five-foot Ryder truck, the measurement being from tip to tail.

Now before this happened, I had been packing boxes for a year, having no idea at all why. However, a voice within, which often talks to me, had told me that I needed to start packing boxes in order to be ready to move at a moment's notice. The idea of doing such a thing at the time did not make good sense. I had been in love with living in Orlando and in Florida in general. I had lived there twelve years and indulged myself in the seafood, the beaches, the seagulls and the beautiful vegetation. My work had been very successful and I had made lifelong friends. The First Presbyterian Church had a fantastic group of ministers and programs and was expanding in order to reach the Orlando population as well as the international visitors who came to the Disney area.

"God," I said, "I have the feeling it is you again, calling me to take up my bed and walk. I'm not sure why because I am so happy here. However, I will pack if you say so. But where would I go? I like it here." But I collected boxes for months and months and soon the garage and family room were piled high. Friends who visited wondered about me. They concluded with a sigh that I was "an original."

I had just returned to Orlando from a winter visit to Montreat and had been amazed at the beauty of the winter days. There the blue sky stood in sharp contrast to the tall, slim, gray, leafless trees, and houses popped out from their usual hidden nooks and crannies and hung splendidly from the edges of the hills and mountains. People walked around in light sweaters on many winter days. Best of all, nature stood out in all its glory, unfettered by crowds of tourists and honking horns. I had visited in the home of a friend who had enthusiastically told me of her delight in living in Montreat all year long. She suggested that I move to Montreat. The thought had never entered my mind. After all, how would I make a living and what would I do all winter? I had earlier imagined the natives to be like bears who climbed into caves and slept away the winter. I was greeted with gales of laughter. "It's just the opposite," my friend stated. "We are busier than ever in the winter and just love it." By the time I got back to Orlando, I had talked myself into what God had probably been planning for years for me. The boxes were packed and I was all ready to go. I just hadn't known where He was sending me.

The morning of the big move, four boys hired by an inexpensive temporary service, began their task. By the end of the day there wasn't an empty spot left in the truck. I paid the boys, waved good-bye to neighbors and climbed high into the enormous truck that dwarfed the tree-lined homes in my neighborhood of brick streets, and quaint, colorful wooden homes that nestled around an L-shaped lake. There was great sadness in my heart because leaving my beloved Florida didn't make sense to me. However, when God said, "Go," I went. There was no denying that this was destined to be. He had some reason; he had a purpose for sending me to Montreat. At the last, when I showed reluctance, He helped me by closing doors that had been opened for many years. I didn't tell my friends that I was leaving until I reached North Carolina, nor did I quit my job, nor try to sell my house. I was clinging to what I knew and loved.

Well, as in all new experiences, I felt pangs of anticipation and not a little trepidation about driving the monster truck. My purse, bursting with last minute unpacked items sat next to me on the seat as well as my two hyperactive poodles that insisted on sitting in my lap as I drove. There was also dog food and a big pan of water that kept spilling as the truck bumped over the brick streets. I noted that a great many cars seemed to swerve away from my direction as they noticed an over middle-aged, more like a senior citizen maneuvering a big, almost unmanageable truck through the narrow neighborhood streets. I honked loudly to scare them and to give them an increased respect for my job and for their need to keep a large margin between them and myself.

On the way out of town, I decided to stop by my office to pick up some files. The office was in downtown Orlando and rush hour had started. I ignored the curses and finger motions of disgruntled motorists and tried to concentrate on the job at hand. I pulled into the driveway of my office building which was next to a restaurant with a big red and white striped awning. But in maneuvering the narrow drive, I misjudged the size of the truck and hit the awning with a bang. Just then I saw customers pouring out in shocked disbelief, running for their lives, not knowing whether a bomb had hit or an earthquake had occurred. People were pointing at me. Some looked terrified. Soon I heard the sirens of a police car, and it didn't take me long to discover where they were going. I think I had heard the very same sirens in my dreams during the restless night that I entertained before I started on this trip to Montreat. Some people would call it "premonition" or maybe in this case it should have been called "predestination" because I felt God was in on a lot of the planning. Of course, when things didn't always go smoothly, I will have to take the blame. My genes have always been loaded in the direction of "if anything can go wrong, it certainly will."

Now, back to the policeman, the fallen awning and the truck which incidentally, got hung up on the beautiful rock garden wall that stood three feet high on the side of the restaurant. The truck's back wheel was caught three feet up in the air and the truck wouldn't go forward or go backward. I won't go into the lengthy details now but I will tell you what happened here was a preview of things to come. All that about the police, the moving violation ticket, the unhappy declarations of the restaurant owner and the tears I shed left me with a certain sense of inadequacy. However, the thought continued to stay with me and to keep things in perspective was that after all, I had graduated from Agnes Scott College and gone to graduate school and the professors along the way had always told us that the world could be ours. We were capable of doing anything that we wanted to do in life. So here I was and this was real life.

As I drove, the pups looked up at me adoringly and licked the tears from my cheeks. The love and acceptance of a person's pets has always reminded me of the boundless acceptance of God. The truck was carrying 12,000 pounds and there was no telling what that van weighed by itself, stripped and naked of cargo. Speaking of the van's actual weight, I would have found this all out if I had stopped earlier at the Weight Station in Florida. When questioned by the state trooper as to why I hadn't pulled into the trucker's weight station, I told him that I had not honestly thought of myself as a bona fide truck driver and that the

Orlando policeman had said nothing about weight stations when he pointed my truck in the direction of North Carolina and said, "Go!" I told him most of the rest of the story, too, and he thought it all so incredible that he let me go free!

By the time I reached the halfway mark to my Montreat destination, it was late in the evening, I was near the outskirts of Savannah, having safely guided the truck through the horrendous traffic of Jacksonville. Now, the classical music on the radio was soothingly putting me in jeopardy of going to sleep before I reached the motel. The dogs were asleep and quiet, and I had very little strength left after the assorted experiences of the day. I stopped at an easy access motel and involved the clerk in giving me a room that was close to where I had parked the moving van. As I looked from my second story room, I could plainly see the huge yellow van, gleaming in the reflected lights of the motel. The tapes that played in my head kept me from sleeping. They played mother's repeated warnings to me concerning the many times that thieves have waited at a motel for an unsuspecting driver to take a room for the night. Then, she said, those thieves would jimmy the lock and take off with the truck and everything you owned. Once in a while in life, her ominous warnings had come true. This might be the time.

At one o'clock in the morning, after a time of fitful sleeping, I dressed and climbed aboard the van again, greatly relieved that it was still parked in the lot when I returned. Soon, I was headed into the deep midnight blue of the early morning. Only *we* truck drivers seemed to be out on the road, and I was grateful for the anonymity of the dark. The other drivers had seemed to find some kind of delight in blowing horns and whistles and playing leap frog with my van. They had seemed as delighted as a pack of wild dogs to find a timid yellow rabbit in their midst.

It was 7:30 AM when I reached the Montreat gate, and *thankfully I remembered to go around the narrow stone gate rather than through it.* Carefully, I began the steep winding road up to my waiting log home. I was within one mountain block of my destination and centered directly in the middle of the road on the straight up slope of Mississippi Road where the nose of one's vehicle points almost straight up toward Heaven. Then, before I could breathe a sigh of relief and before I could thank God for safely delivering me to my home, the truck stopped...dead. It wouldn't move forward; nor would it move backward. I tugged on the heavy handle of the emergency brake, but at first was afraid to get out of the truck for fear it would somehow roll backwards into Montreat, destroying everything in its path. I could imagine an even worse incident than the one that had taken place in the rush hour traffic in Orlando.

Out of the corner of my eye, I glimpsed the first sign of life, except for the birds, in the early morning mist of Montreat. A distinguished man in his robe and slippers was descending the front porch steps in order to pick up the morning paper on the road close to my truck. I later found out he was a famous missionary doctor to Korea. I took a deep breath, secured the hand brake even tighter, said another prayer and then climbed down three feet from the truck. The dogs looked worried at my departure. I greeted the man, explaining that I could soon be his new neighbor around the corner. However, at this moment I had a rather large problem to overcome. I asked if I could use his phone, explaining my dilemma.

Now, I told him, the truck had stopped dead in the middle of the road and I expected that something terrible had happened to the engine. It was pretty obvious to an observer that there was a problem. The nice man invited me to come into the home and have coffee with him and with his wife. He stated that he thought we could work out the problems inside the house where it was much warmer. The month was February. That cold fact had been the least of my worries.

Just as we sat down and started to drink the coffee, Maury, the right hand man for Ruth and Billy, my other neighbors-to-be, knocked on the door and implored one of us to move the truck if possible because it was blocking the road. He was in a rush to take Ruth to the airport. Time was of the essence. I promised to do my best to find help and began to make a series of phone calls while Maury went up the mountain to pick up Ruth. When he came back with her fifteen minutes later, the van was still in the middle of the road. Maury had to carefully maneuver the car onto a dangerous drop off shoulder of the road. I later heard that he broke his automobile antenna in doing so.

Meanwhile, I called a former Sunday school teacher from my church in Orlando. He was now the President of Montreat College and was the only man I knew in the valley at the time before I had met David, the doctor who gave me coffee. I woke Bill up. It was only 7:30 AM on a Saturday morning. I asked for his sage, manly advice on the topic of broken down trucks. I thanked him for this advice and apologized for the early call but related that I was certain he would be concerned about the safety of Montreat as I was. (The truck as a missile would have a powerful effect on anything in its path.) He suggested a Ryder tow truck. After thanking him and hanging up, I called Ryder's emergency service. They promised to come at once. They had evidently been to Montreat before. Directions weren't a problem. When the driver of the tow truck arrived one-half hour later and ascertained the situation, he turned to me and said in some disbelief and amazement, "Lady, yah'll don't need no towin'! Ya'll is plumb out of gas."

With that he proceeded to get permission to siphon some gas from the car of my new host. He filled my truck with a quarter tank of gas and I was off to my home just around the corner. I later sold the doctor's home for him in a sort of "thank you action" for his good will toward me that morning.

A Frist First and Last—The B and B Experience

"I have learned to be satisfied with the things I have and with every-thing that happens. I know how to live when I am poor and I know how to live when I have plenty. I have learned to secret of being happy at any time in everything that happens. I can do all things through Christ, because he gives me strength."

—Philippians 4:11–13 (NCV)

Jane's B and B in Mama's log cabin.

When I first arrived in Montreat, I was not at all certain as to how I would earn a living. I had hoped to paint and to write, but I knew that those endeavors alone would not put food on the table. So, I decided to turn five rooms of my small log cabin into bedrooms and to invite guests to enjoy the stream and rustic surroundings in the environment of a bed and breakfast. I lovingly decorated the rooms with unique antiques. I put colorful quilts on the beds and placed brass lanterns on the bedside tables to light up the dark corners of the log house. The large decks were filled to overflowing with comfortable lounge chairs and swings. I was overjoyed that the stream was tumbling close by the porch and that it would be a catalyst to lull my guests into a state of euphoria while they were enjoying their experience at my bed and breakfast.

I advertised in major Presbyterian magazines as well as through the Mountain Retreat Association. It was not long until I was overwhelmed with calls for reservations.

The only problem with this dream was that I gave little thought to the "breakfast" part of the advertised bed and breakfast. I was certainly not known in any circle as an old fashioned cook! It was not that I could not cook. I just did not often take the time to do it correctly as I had done in the days when my children were small. The night before my first guests came, I ran to the grocery store and bought six kinds of bran cereals, some assorted bagels, all kinds of fruit and some egg beaters. I even bought regular old eggs and bacon. I felt that now I was adequately prepared for all kinds of tastes.

My first reservation had been made by a delightful young college girl who was graduating from Montreat College that very spring. She wanted to give her mother, grandmother and aunt a gift in gratitude for her college experience. However, she added that she did not have much money, and she asked if I would give a rather large discount. Since I imagined that there might be a few kinks in my operation at the beginning of its experience, I agreed to take off two thirds from the total price. I told her that her family might be considered the first guinea pigs in my bed and breakfast. She did not seem to mind. She was pleased with the whole arrangement, and I was soon happily on my way to being a bonafide bed and breakfast proprietor.

The day of my opening came and the guests arrived. I suppose it was because of the request for the discount that I was somewhat surprised to see her family arrive in a large, late model Cadillac. However, the group was such a delightful one and their joy was so catching, that I was also caught up in the spirit of their vacation. They all unpacked and quickly adjourned to the deck. They talked for hours and sang beloved old camp songs and well known spirituals. I visited with them for quite awhile, but in time I felt I was needed elsewhere to do other bed and breakfast types of tasks. By 9:00 PM I had begun to feel very sleepy. I was accustomed to arising at 3:00 AM almost daily. I was able to work on my computer, write letters and paint during these early hours when the phone did not ring.

So, on this first night of my B&B endeavor, I went to bed about 9:00 PM and fell into a deep sleep. A quiet, but persistent knock startled me from my sleep. "I'm sorry to bother you," the voice stated, "but the commode will not flush." I groggily climbed out of bed, threw on my robe and attended to the problem at hand. In the years of living alone, I had become rather adept at small problems concerning plumbing and electrical matters. While I was up, I decided to wash my hair and then I went back to an even deeper sleep. Suddenly, there was a loud knock at the door and a soft apology for disturbing me a second time. The voice from the other side of the door explained that the bed had fallen in. My hair was still half wet and my eyes were half closed as I went into the guest room, dropped to all fours, studied the problem under the bed and then turned and lay on my back and scooted under the half fallen antique four poster. The carpenter, in his haste to complete some work, had inadvertently pushed back the slats toward the foot of the bed, leaving a big, empty space under the mattress. When my guest climbed into the bed, the mattress had tipped like a seesaw, depositing her squarely on the floor. At this point, I knew I would have to do some fast repairs in order for the guest (and me!) to get a good night's rest. While under the bed, I lifted the whole mattress with my feet and carefully manipulated the slats back into their proper position. Then I was off to bed, once again. There were, happily, no more knocks for the rest of the night.

The next morning, however, meant breakfast needed to be served. I arose early in order to greet the guests with hot coffee. When they dressed, they sat down at the table. I went through the list of the food that I had gathered from the grocery store, fully confident that there were ample choices. Much to my amazement, nothing on my list sounded appetizing or appealing to my guests. Not one of them was fond of any of the six types of bran cereal, nor did they want bacon, eggs, or bagels. I quickly pondered what I could do to make them happy. Suddenly, a bright idea come to me, I remembered the dogs' special cabinet. In it was a special box of Cocoa Puffs that I gave them occasionally, though not often, as it had too much sugar and would lead to dental problems. I asked the guests, "Do you like Cocoa Puffs?" They responded in unison that they loved them. Happily, from that moment on, breakfast was a success!

However, the memory of that first breakfast failure at the beginning, and the thought of future breakfasts where I might end up trying to please hundreds of different palates, sent me into a tailspin of thinking. I could just see myself spending future hours in the kitchen, rolling and patting dough in a powdery apron. I could picture myself leaning down endless numbers of times with my head in the oven, testing the doneness of a variety of homemade quiches and breakfast rolls. Oh my, was I frightened now! My thoughts leapt ahead to a variety of possible solutions.

As the guests were departing, I hesitatingly asked them for their suggestions for improvements. I dreaded to hear their list. However, to my surprise, they all agreed that the time at my home had been a huge success. Their only suggestion was this: "You should take photos of the various rooms and have the photos made into post cards so that visitors can take them home as a souvenir of their stay with you…After all, your place is so charming!"

As their car rolled out of sight, I dropped my arm at my side, tired from having enthusiastically waved goodbye. My mouth was weak from smiling for so many hours. Just as I came back into the house, the phone rang and a voice on the other end of the line asked to make a reservation for bed and breakfast. I quickly answered, with no hesitation, "How about bed without *breakfast*?" My caller responded that it would be fine with her, as she was not accustomed to breakfast. However, she stated, she knew of several eating places that she would like to try if she were ever hungry in the early morning.

So, as a result of this enlightening conversation, I became the proprietor of a new type of B and B. It was a B and B with only one B!

Jane resting after a harried day at the B and B.

Jarvis

*"Trust in the Lord with all thy heart and lean not to thy own under-
standing, in all thy ways acknowledge Him and He will direct thy
path."*

—*Proverbs 3:5*

This is the car and RV Jane took to Florida with Jarvis

One fall afternoon in Montreat when the sun was out warming the countryside
and the leaves were like shimmering gold, my sister Charlotte and I decided to
take a little outing and visit a large RV facility about thirty miles from home. We
had no intention of buying anything. It was just fun to look at all the different
styles of RVs. I had talked of wanting to own a motor home for years, but it was
just talk. We had a wonderful time "just looking" but as I think back to that
afternoon, I often wonder why it was I who came home with the motor home
and not my sister. She had an easy way of talking me into buying one. I didn't

know what hit me until I was on the way to Florida. Later I discovered that she had wanted one herself but felt safer talking me into buying one. She always learned from her older sister's mistakes and moved rather smoothly through life.

After a few days went by, I took one of my friends, Mary, along to hear the explanations of the technical man at the RV center as he explained the electrical and plumbing systems. I didn't want to miss anything and I thought she would be a good backup if I ever needed help. However, when things broke down later on my trip, she wasn't there to remind me of what the man had said and what I was to do about any problems. I was on my own. I assured myself that I would be perfectly safe because I had, by now, driven nine moving vans in and the around the USA in the past.

Only a month after buying it, I decided to make some use of the motor home. The weather was getting cold in my area of North Carolina. Florida became my obvious destination. After all, I had two sons living there and would be able to visit them on my way through Florida.

It was rather exciting to begin packing summer clothes, plastic dishes, cameras and bathing suits. I came up with a brilliant thought. I would take two bicycles, one for a man one for a woman. They would be balanced on a bike rack on the back. I had been warned that I might be in danger driving alone as a single woman, I figured that this plan with the bicycles for both genders would discourage any possible kidnapping of a helpless woman. Then I had an even more brilliant idea. I would "build" a man to ride in the passenger seat beside me, just like the one I had placed on the bed of my teacher in prep school.

My passenger turned out to look so real that when anyone saw a photo of him sitting beside me in the RV, one thought he was a real person. He was dressed in blue jeans and a blue jean jacket, rust colored leather gloves and rust leather boots to match. With my help, he put his leg on the dashboard and held a map in one hand while propping his right arm up on the armrest under the right hand window. Thanks to the rubber industry, I anointed his PV pipe shoulders (hidden under the blue jeans jacket) with a perfectly handsome head which was an exact copy of Regis (remember Regis and Kathy Lee). I was able to buy this head which looked like a man of about sixty years old from a costume store for only $19.00. This was a small amount to pay for safety during my travels.

Jarvis, Jane and poodles in the RV.

As mentioned before, the passenger in the RV looked so real that I decided to name him. He was so unusual that I decided to name him an unusual name: "Jarvis." After I left on the trip, my brother Tommy went to a Christmas party and happened to take a picture of Jarvis and me with him to the party. As he was showing it, someone asked what he thought of his sister's new boyfriend. He teasingly answered, "I think he is a dummy and a stuffed shirt." His friend was shocked at the response and showed it on his face. My brother explained and they all had a good laugh.

I had been warned by others that it was dangerous to park anywhere but at an RV Park, so I was very nervous when I pulled into a free Cracker Barrel parking lot for the evening. Cracker Barrel encourages this as it draws customers for dinner and breakfast. After dinner I made sure that the RV was parked under a bright light for safety and then nervously turned off the inside lights and climbed into bed, shuddering at each sound outside the RV. At least the door had a double lock, I felt and that was safety in itself.

Jarvis resting in the RV.

In the morning, breathing easily now as I had experienced a safe night, I began to look for the keys in order to go for breakfast. They were nowhere to be found. Panic! As I climbed down the stairs and opened the door, I heard a jangle. Guess where the keys were? They were hanging right on the door outside under the bright light. They had been there all night! This was my first safety lesson of the trip. Never leave the keys outside the van unless you are with them. When I arrived at the next filling station, I bought a chain, which fitted on a belt and kept the keys attached at all times.

Leaving the station, I miscalculated the distance to the side of the road and the two right tires sunk into the ditch filled with water, and turned over the RV. Luckily, it was kept from falling flat by a fence. It took three hours for the emergency truck to pull us out.

After driving a total of about 560 miles from North Carolina without any other mishaps, I stopped for a visit in Orlando to see a friend. Because his car was being serviced, he rode in the van with me to get some beer for himself at an ABC store. While I sat in the van in front of the bright light of the store, he went inside. I looked over at Jarvis and noted that during the long trip, he had sunk down as his insides compacted somewhat and he was leaning out the window, rather askew, and grinning in his same old way. He never changed his expression.

When my friend came back into the van, he said, with a big laugh, "That clerk said he wasn't going to sell me any beer. I answered, 'Why not? I'm of age.' The clerk said me, 'Since you have already gotten that passenger in the van so drunk, it might be dangerous to be out tonight.'" The next day I went to Wal-Mart and bought a small ironing board, which I placed down the back of Jarvis' shirt and pants. This action brought him up to a height that made him seem sober and six feet tall.

Now, I was well on the way to my destination in South Florida. There had been no major problems, and I was two thirds of the way and feeling much more certain that I could handle anything.

Whoops!

When I arrived at an RV park that allowed me bring dogs, I went into the office, paid for a nice spot under a shade tree and headed toward my number 123 spot. I had never backed an RV before and was taking quite some time trying to edge in between two RVs, which looked as if they were worth at least $200,000 each. An elderly Englishman came tearing out of his RV, waving his hands frantically in the air. He shouted, "Have you ever backed an RV before?" I said, "Never!" "Can I help you?" he asked. Of course I was delighted for help of any kind. After he waved me to the right and then to the left and showed me which way to crank the steering wheel (at least a dozen times), he helped me hook up the water, the electricity, the plumbing and the TV.

I was so grateful for his help and turned to him and said, "Thank you so much for all you have done to help me!"

He answered, "Well, lady, I saw that you needed help since you have a disabled husband in the front seat."

The following morning, when I strolled around to look at the park where I planned to stay for a couple months, I was amused to see that everyone had their own little world wrapped around their particular RV. Awnings sported Christmas lights, wooden or steel pink flamingos held nameplates in their mouths, with signs saying everything from "The Jensens of Canada" to "Denny and Laurie, retired and ready to go." A big metal shovel stuck in the ground in front of a palm tree said, "Rust in Peace."

After my travels across the country in all kinds of situations one thing I have found is that not only does God provide help in times of trouble, but He sends good Samaritans in many forms and shapes.

FLORIDA

To waken every morning
Where the birds have come and stayed
To waken every morning
Where the spring has yet to fade,
Such joy invades the spirit
With such a life as this…
To live in Florida's winter
Is to live a life of bliss!

SPRING QUICKLY

It's that time of year again
That tripping, floating, hopping time
When warm breezes catch at silken hair
And push about without a care.

It's the time when wishes dance
Through flowering paths and fluffy skies
The sounds of brooks and calls of birds
Fulfill our unexpressed words.

It's the time when perfumes drop
So heavily laden on the air
And naught cuts through their lined folds
Unless the eyes of human souls.

Soft now, a voice, hear it—
It comes quietly through the blowing grass
Whispering, chattering, laughing, singing
Ever through the stillness ringing.

O, heavens, smile a little longer
Stay changeless but to beam or spark
Throw not thick showers or quick start
Upon this gentle, human heart.

Laugh gaily, little one, today.
Spring's promises never hold or stay
Catch stars and buds without delay
For sudden is the end of May.

The Poodles

o o o o o o o o o o o o o o o o o o o o o o o o o o o o o o o o o
"A merry heart doeth good."

—*Proverbs 17:22*

For seventeen years I was blessed to have two little white poodles, a three pound Teacup poodle, Buffy, and a six pound Toy poodle, Rascal. They were born in my bed since their mother, Lindy, another Toy poodle, slept with me every night. I never realized that she was pregnant so it was a real surprise when they were born. I had owned the two large dogs in Denver that I spoke about earlier. Poodles had never been dogs I thought I would desire. However, when a friend, Jeannine, needed me to take her dog Lindy for a year, while she lived in Jamaica, I agreed to do it. Little by little I fell in love with this breed of dog. These two baby dogs, Rascal and Buffy, started going with me to work, to play, to church and to travel. They were so good that when they were placed in a black mesh bag, the size of a large purse, they knew that they were to be quiet and never bark. They were fantastic in understanding this. If they needed to go to the bathroom, they would make a tiny sound, like a murmured "grrr" and I immediately knew what they needed and I would respond appropriately. Out they would pop when I unzipped the bag and then jump obediently right back in after doing their business.

One summer day I was traveling in my car from Orlando to North Carolina and stopped at a restaurant in order to have a bite of food to break the long trip. It was too hot to leave the dogs in the car so I took their bag on my arm and carried them with me into the restaurant. I put the bag on the seat beside me in the booth and waited for the waitress to come along. I ordered stir-fry chicken. Both the dogs and I liked that dish. Just as the waitress was taking my order, I heard a "grrr" sound and knew that the dogs needed to go to the bathroom. The waitress looked at me in a startled way. I quickly rubbed my stomach and said, "Please hurry with my food. My stomach is growling."

Poodles enjoy their dog bag.

Another day when I planned to leave the dogs in the car with the windows down and go to church, I noticed that it was warmer than I had expected and so either I had to leave church and take the dogs home or take them into church with me in the zipped up bag. As they were nearly always quiet, I didn't feel too worried about their making a sound. Through the first twenty minutes, they were as quiet as mice. When I went into church, I failed to remember I had given them a leftover hamburger patty from a restaurant where I had gone for breakfast. As the violin began to play the lovely, joyous offertory, Rascal and Buffy got into an unusual dogfight over the hamburger patty that I had given them from our Denny's breakfast, shaking the bag from side to side and growling and barking. I am sure that the whole church congregation had never heard anything like it in their church experience and everyone was turning around staring in my direction. My sister and her husband who were seated next to me looked very uncomfortable and tried with body language to distance themselves from me. They looked the other way. I leaned over and whispered to one of the teenagers seated on my other side and asked her if she would take the bag outside and put it under a shady bush until church was over. She seemed extremely willing to take her leave of the long service and left immediately with bag in hand. She chose to play outside with them until church was over.

During the seventeen years of owning Rascal and Buffy, there were numerous incidents where I had interesting encounters with the mesh bag, the dogs and other people. However, in Orlando, I could not leave them at home because I had a zero lot line home that was close to the neighbors and they complained at the slightest sound from the dogs.

On this particular occasion, I was about forty minutes from home in Orlando and very close to Disney World. I was running errands and delivering contracts to an office in the southern area of Orlando. As I was pulling out of the parking lot of an office where I had been, I noticed a bus the size of a Greyhound bus, loading people who were in a long line by the bus. The bus had big black Mickey Mouse ears sticking out the top and paintings all over the side advertising Mickey and Disney World. I went up to the bus and asked the hostess, "What is going on?"

She answered, "Come and join us. This is a free trip to Disney to the opening of their new Caribbean Hotel. There will be a tour of the facilities, refreshments and music. We will come back in a couple of hours." I had been hearing about this new resort and wanted to see it. However, there was no time to take a forty minute trip home to deposit the dogs. The car was again too hot for the dogs to stay there.

Grabbing the zipped up dog bag and a black sweater that I used in Florida air-conditioning, I joined the enthusiastic crowd and followed at the end of the line. We rode a few minutes, arrived at the resort and as we got off the bus, men in tuxedos greeted us. An orchestra was playing by the front entrance. Into the big lounge we went and then followed the hostess down numerous halls to the brand new bedrooms decorated in colors appropriate for the Caribbean. We wandered through room after room and Rascal and Buffy remained quiet. After an hour of the tour, I was certain by now they would be hungry, thirsty and restless for a bathroom break. Seeing the refreshments offered by the resort, I took a paper plate full of chocolate chip cookies and lemonade and headed for the stall in the restroom where I gave the dogs the cookies and lemonade. It was then that I realized a problem was ahead. Where would I take the dogs for the bathroom?

Leaving the tour, I walked outside to the newly planted palms and red flowered bushes and tried to find a spot where attendants and people were scarce. In seconds the dogs were back in the bag and ready to go on with the tour. Soon the bus returned to pick us up and we all climbed back on the bus. I was sitting next to a single man at the back of the bus. I had placed the bag on my lap and I had spread my black sweater over the bag and up to my neck. As we drove along, the bag began to move under the sweater, rolling right and left. By now the dogs were restless as they had enjoyed a two-hour tour and not made a sound. As my sweater rolled like the ocean, the man next to me peered down at the moving sweater and said, "When is the baby due?"

I responded, "Any minute now!" Thank goodness we stopped, the doors opened and we all climbed off the bus and went to our respective cars.

Jane and her poodles in their backpack on one of her trips.

The Club

○ ○
"If a man digs a pit, he will fall into it."

—Proverbs 26:27

In my older years I joined one of the national clubs that was formerly a men's club only. At the time I joined, it had been welcoming women for a few years. There were a few women members but mostly about seventy men. It was a fine time of fellowship, food and good works for others. I found that the strictness about being on time in order to have the Pledge of Allegiance was difficult for me. My pool aerobics and the meeting of the club were overlapping. It was too difficult to change from a wet bathing suit at the pool and get to the restaurant looking calm and settled in time for the Pledge.

On the day of the last meeting I ever attended, I rushed to get dressed too fast. I put on my full turquoise skirt and blouse rather quickly. As I was walking across the parking lot at the restaurant, I recognized one of the men from the group, beckoning me to come over to his car. I didn't know him except by sight. "Miss, Miss," he said, "would you come over here a minute, please." In any other town I would not have gone toward him. I would have marched as fast as I could into the restaurant and away from him. I was lucky that I did not do that at this time. He said, "I hate to have to tell you this, but your dress is tucked up in your panty-hose in the back. I didn't think you would want to go into the restaurant like that!" You can be sure that he had warned me about something I had not known about. I was saved from facing at least eighty people half undressed.

After this very embarrassing incident I was telling my friend Gigi the details. It didn't occur to me that she would be asked to speak in front of the same group. She was often asked to speak all around the United States, but her subjects were usually on God and family. We were having dinner at her home one evening, when she casually announced that she had used me as an illustration in her speech that very day at the club. She said, "I told the men of the club that I felt right at home with them, as I had already been introduced to them by a friend's earlier experience." She elaborated on the story that I had told her and she probably exaggerated as well. In shock and chagrin, I resigned from the club before I had to face the members again.

The Library Card and Other Stories

At the Black Mountain Library one morning I overheard a tiny elderly lady arguing with the librarian at the front desk. She did not feel that she should have to pay for a library card when she was only going to visit the town for two weeks. She said that she was staying at the hotel next door and could be trusted to return any book she borrowed when she finished reading it. Her distress at hearing the rules was very evident. I stepped up to the desk and asked the lady librarian if the visitor could use my library card to check books out during those two weeks. She smiled and nodded yes to me.

The little lady grabbed both my hands and squeezed them as her way of thanking me. "Oh, my dear," she cried out, "you are wonderful to do that for me. I am Mrs. Smith from Sanford, Florida. What is your name, dear?" When I told her my name, Jane Frist, she questioned me excitedly, "Would you have ever known a John Chester Frist?"

"I certainly would. He was my Dad!" I said. Then she pulled me aside, away from the main desk, and she began to relay to me that she and my Aunt, Helen, were best friends as little children in Meridian, Mississippi, some ninety years before. She and I would have stood there the rest of the day as she related one story after another, but I suggested that she check out the books that she might want using my card and that we could then go to some place to eat and continue the stories.

This new friendship turned into a five-year friendship until she died in her late 90s. We met every year when she came up to North Carolina for vacation and I even visited her home in Florida and tried to give her suggestions that would help her to sell her classic Spanish style home built in the 1920s. She told me stories about my grandparents and their children that I would never have known otherwise. One time my Aunt Helen and this little lady, Charlotte, had been in a horse and buggy with my grandfather when they were very young. The little girls had stayed in the buggy while my grandfather went inside a store to pick up something. The horse broke lose and tore down the street with the children clinging to the carriage for dear life. It was a lucky thing that someone stopped the runaway horse and saved the little girls.

Charlotte remembered playing paper dolls with my aunt. She also told me how the two little girls held their skirts wide as they stood in front of the beveled glass door of the big Victorian home where my father grew up. The girls were trying to protect my father as a small boy from the streetcar viewers as he drank goats' milk from a bottle. Goats' milk saved his life, as he had been deathly ill from drinking regular milk. Charlotte remembered my grandfather sitting on a three-legged stool to milk the goats. It seemed unusual to her to have goats in the backyard of a seven bedroom Victorian home right near the center of Meridian.

The most interesting story was the one that I already knew but it was fascinating to hear her tell it. My grandfather had been the Stationmaster of the Meridian railroad station. He had been watching as one of the many trains from New York to New Orleans pulled into the station, bearing down on a woman and her child as they crossed the tracks. He had run out in front of the train, pushing the woman and child off the tracks and saving their lives. As a result, he was critically injured and died as a result of those injuries when my father was only ten years old. He received the United States Medal for Lifesaving on the railroad, a very important Medal given for Heroes. It was given by the government of the United States and was awarded through the Interstate Commerce Commission under Act of Congress 23. As a result of the death of their father, my father and his six-year-old brother, Tommy, the future founder of Hospital Corporation of America, began working early in life to help their mother as she struggled to bring up her four children alone. The luxurious seven-bedroom home had to be turned into a rooming house for young men who were studying to be doctors. My uncle was so inspired by the young doctors that when he grew up, he also became a doctor. My father was inspired to become a minister. Their goals in life were to help others to be well in body and in mind. Uncle Tommy's patients and Daddy's flock loved these caring men very deeply.

Uncle Tommy and Aunt Dorothy

"Be very careful how you live. Do not live like those who are not wise, but live wisely. Use every chance you have for doing good, because these are evil times."

—*Ephesians 5:15, 16 (NCV)*

There was quite a difference in the income of the two brothers. My Uncle Tommy always made sure that he stuffed a few dollars in our pockets when we were children as the minister's family struggled to make ends meet. When we were adults, he and his wife Dorothy saw to it that the minister's family was helped through some of the more difficult financial situations such as surgery, weddings and other problems. Uncle Tommy was ardent about the work ethic as he had worked so hard himself when he was young putting himself through college, parking cars, driving students from the train, taking laundry of the students to the cleaners, waiting tables and so forth. While I struggled to make a living and to grow as I learned from difficult situations, he never stopped the struggle, but would often reward me with a nice gift for trying so hard. He never wanted money to discourage my work ethic.

During our vacations we would often visit Uncle Tommy and Aunt Dorothy's home in Nashville. Aunt Dorothy would take us to the corner drugstore and tell us that we could each buy something special. She would take Charlotte and me to a lovely dress shop and let us choose a special dress. Their home was the center of entertainment for the whole neighborhood. Anyone who wanted to play tennis on their courts or swim in the Frist pool was welcome. My aunt would come out on the porch and call out, "Aren't we having fun?" she would bring out sandwiches and cokes, cake and ice cream. There were two refrigerators in order to hold enough food for the family of seven and the entire visiting neighborhood. If she heard that a neighbor child fell out of a tree, or that someone was ill, she would send over a turkey or even pay for their medical help if the neighbor's family couldn't afford it. Once she furnished a whole Orphans' Home with air-conditioning and told the AC company manager not to tell anyone that the gift was from her. There were hundreds of incidents like this. Uncle Tommy was also always thinking of others. He built hospitals, retirement homes and nursing homes. He gave money for scientific and medical research. He served for many years, volunteering to examine medical missionaries going overseas.

Uncle Tommy and Aunt Dorothy always praised their five children, three boys and two girls. They gave them the confidence that each of them could do anything in life that they wanted. They emphasized that they should help others in whatever field they chose. As a result the three boys all became doctors. Tommy, Jr. started HCA with Uncle Tommy's help, Bobby was a great heart surgeon and Bill became an unusually brilliant heart-lung transplant surgeon. This latter child, Bill, was so accustomed to hearing his mother calling Senators and Congressmen on the phone and telling them how she thought they should run the country that he developed a deep interest in politics along with his passion for medicine. When I asked him why he was leaving his fine career as a transplant surgeon in order to run for the Senate, he answered, "Because I can help more people."

Cousin Bill at 16 visiting Jane in Colorado.

The Accessory Building

o o o o o o o o o o o o o o o o o o o o o o o o o o o o o o o

"I will lie down and sleep in peace, for you alone, O Lord, make me dwell in safety."

—*Psalm 4:8*

Since my log cabin was the basic log cabin that Mama put together in the early 50s, it was supposed to be a summer cottage; it therefore had very little insulation. It was also only 800 square feet in the beginning. Year by year I added a little here and there. However, there came a time when the mountain and the stream (being right up against the house) would not allow any further expansion. I decided I had to add a building about fifteen or twenty feet up the mountain from the original log cabin. Because of Montreat zoning regulations, I had to sign a paper stating that the new structure could only be used for an art studio, storage and a "place to rest." I would not be allowed to spend the night there.

One day after it was newly built, I fell hard while going down the twenty steps to the main log cabin and sprained my ankle. In order to be close to the car, I stayed overnight in the Accessory Building, lying uncomfortably in a wing chair, a "place to rest," until my ankle was better. Within days I received a letter from the zoning administrator of the town who was overly diligent in interpreting the law concerning building codes in our little town. She sent me a written notice warning me that I could be put in jail or be forced to pay a $500 a day fine for every day that I had been in the cabin illegally. I was not supposed to sleep there. This zoning administrator had probably never sent out a letter like the one she sent me, and after this probably never sent another. I had a question that I might have asked her if I had talked to her after receiving the letter, "Can you please tell me where this town jail is located?" None of us who lived in the town knew of a jail nearby. I certainly didn't want to leave money in my will at my death to have a jail built in memory of me.

I often left the white curly haired poodles in the Accessory Building watching the TV show "Animal Planet." Many times I used this little building as a dog-house. Looking from a distance the light haired elderly dogs in the faint light of the TV could have been confused with an elderly blonde lady, resting in the wing chair. Anyway, though the authorities never picked me up and took me to jail, I got the point of the letter and made sure that I didn't even rest in the Accessory Building again, much less live there. In the future, I just used it for storage. Had the rules of the town not been so stringent, I as a single woman living on a half acre could have been able to sleep on my own property, whether it is in one building or the other. I was never one for unreasonable rules. Remember my kindergarten experience!

Hezekiah

"The Lord giveth and the Lord taketh away. Blessed be the name of the Lord."

—*Job 1:21*

One afternoon my friend Ruth asked me if I could find her a baby Lab to give to her husband, Billy for Christmas. She had heard me say that my brother had just bought a very smart little dog from a breeder in Tennessee. Ruth and Bill had always loved dogs and had numerous breeds over the years. When we were growing up, the most beloved and memorable dog that they owned was called Belshazzar, a large St. Bernard from Switzerland. He was so large and friendly that the children would all ride him like riding a horse, dress him in clothes and roll with him on the lawn. So when I called my brother, Johnny, to purchase a smart puppy like the one he had just bought for himself, he was delighted to do it. He drove to a little town several hours below Nashville to pick up the dog. While he was driving home with the new baby dog in his lap, he received a cell phone call saying that his wife had just died suddenly from an aneurysm.

Our family all gathered in Nashville for the Memorial Service during the next few days and the little pup was lovingly passed from one hand to the other of family members until it was time to go back to Montreat with the Christmas gift for Bill. Two days before the funeral my brother Tommy called our brother Johnny in Nashville and asked, "What is the name of the dog?" In all the confusion of the events surrounding the planning of the memorial service, he had forgotten to ask.

Bill with Hezekiah

Johnny said that the puppy had been named Hezekiah since Bill and Ruth's other dogs seemed to have Biblical names. Then Johnny said, "Hezekiah is the book with my favorite verse in the Bible. I'll bet you haven't read it."

Then Tommy, thinking Johnny meant the Bible, said, "Oh, yes, I read it all the time."

Johnny laughed and said, "Go read Hezekiah 3:13 and tell me what it says." He chuckled to himself thinking he had pulled a fast one on his brother, knowing that there was no book of Hezekiah in the Bible. He waited for the ensuing phone call from Tommy. It came within fifteen minutes.

Tommy said, "I read 3:13 of Hezekiah and it said, 'Thou shall not make a fool of thy brother."

Christmas morning came and I met Tommy at his home in order to go with him to take the precious puppy up the mountain to Ruth. Tommy had dressed the pup in a large red Christmas bow appropriate for the big occasion. We wanted to be there to see Bill's reaction to his special Christmas gift. He was delighted. After returning home, I waited about five days before calling Bill to ask him how he was enjoying the Christmas gift. He answered that though he loved the little dog, he was afraid that it wasn't going to work out to have such a rambunctious pup that still had to be trained. He was afraid of tripping over the dog and falling, as he was already a bit shaky on his feet. I called Johnny to ask if we could return the dog, telling him that Bill was thinking of giving the dog to his son Franklin. Johnny had another idea. He wanted the dog himself and was eager to buy it back. He connected the dog's arrival with the loss of his wife. He felt that the dog would be a great comfort to him. He loved dogs as dearly as I loved dogs. I thought that this particular love of dogs must be genetic. I love dogs so much that one day I asked my friend Ruth if she thought that our beloved pets would go to Heaven, she answered that if that is what would give us true happiness, they would be there. God had promised us unbelievable joy in Heaven.

Johnny on his motorcycle with his two passengers.

Johnny left the name "Hezekiah" behind when he became reacquainted with the pup. He then named it Lancelot. After training Lancelot and training his doggie brother, Cedrick, he bought a motorcycle with a sidecar, put red bandanas on the necks of the dogs and goggles over their eyes. He drove around the countryside of the Swannanoa Valley where his vacation home was located. He would pull up to a restaurant, tell the dogs to sit tight and then go in and get a bite to eat. The dogs would stay obediently in the sidecar while crowds would gather to take pictures of the delightful scene. One restaurant owner even offered to let Johnny have a free meal because his dogs were drawing business to the restaurant.

To this day, Johnny enjoys his celebrity because of his association with the dogs as well as his own good looks.

TEMPORARY DESPAIR AT THE DEATH OF A LOVED ONE

The once warm breeze grew
Chill and damp
Against my cheek
A few leaves and papers flew up
And quickly scattered across the grass.
There were no more footsteps.
In the distance faint calls and laughter echoed
From children playing.
With my foot I drew
Pictures in the sand.
I traced the lifeline in my hand.
It dwindled off suddenly and fell short.
I was glad
For he never returned.

DEATH OF A MALE FRIEND

You are dead!
I know it,
But I stand
Before your body
Bearing the pain of wilting memories
The oak trees mourn your going
With drooping branches
Silhouetted against
A sleeting sky.
The cold winds whip my skirt
In useless endeavor to push me from all hurt.
Where are you?
You who lifted me above
The difficulties of life,
Who called me
In joy or strife.
No longer rings your deep voice
Upon the hidden air waves, in circles
Pounding on my soul,
Beckoning me to fly upward
To dizzying heights
Above the sunlit waves!

A GIRLFRIEND'S DEATH

Our dear, dear Ann,
Our precious one
Is present as I write.
Her liveliness and caring ways
Still linger in the night.
Her warm, kind hands
Left fingerprints upon the little Duck[1]
Who sits so gently at the gate
Dispelling love and luck!
She's not gone far,
Just around the bend.
She's gone like all before…
She gone ahead
To see the place
Where God's prepared a room
For all of us who linger here
With pain forever more.
Don't grieve so long
My special friends,
For we will see her soon
It's soon that heaven opens up
And we will meet the Groom.

---

1.   Her home was called "Duck Inn."

DEATH

It hovers near and carries on
The threat of our impending sleep.
Each time another friend is gone
Each time a funeral makes us weep.

We weep for what we had not said
For deeds we planned to do as yet.
For dreams that have not yet come true,
So small our gifts, so big our debt.

We weep for all we promised God,
And haven't worked it in as yet.
We weep for family gone before
Even those we wished we had not met.

We prayed our deeds would never scar
But wonder as we watch our own.
Those days when we were young, so far
Have left us to revise, atone.

Dear God, I know we'll meet some day
And all the folks will gather round.
The music shall be at its best
And lost loved ones will now be found.

So why we weep is still unknown
For promised glories will be shown.
Oh, Hallelujah, no more pain
And life's big mysteries will be known.

Nancy's Death

o o o o o o o o o o o o o o o o o o o o o o o o o o o o o o o o o o
"Though I walk through the valley of the shadow of death, I will fear no evil: for you are with me; your rod and your staff, they comfort me."

—*Psalm 23:4*

When I met Nancy, she was a lady in her early 70s and well known around our town as being forthright and honest. She had definite ideas on everything and didn't mind letting everyone know. She loved to travel, have fun, entertain with tea parties and go to church wearing large colorful picture hats. Not many women chose to wear them in the 90s, but many of us wished we were brave enough to don a lovely chapeau as she did.

One day, Nancy discovered that she had cancer. She traveled to Florida and had treatments. She talked of being afraid of the unknown, of death and of Heaven. She said that she wished that she knew more. So I wrote several pages on my ideas about Heaven. Nancy was thrilled with the papers and made dozens of copies for her friends and even for her doctors. Since she was so pleased with my view of Heaven, I wanted to make her happy again. So I painted a watercolor of her in a big pink picture hat, standing on the side of our Lake Susan and gazing heavenward. Angels were reaching down to her from the sky. I drew another, a line drawing, of angels hovering over the Montreat Gate.

Over the months, Nancy kept on going like the battery rabbit in spite of her cancer. She loved to have teas for her friends, using a different set of pitchers and teacups for each person. She had a large collection of unique china. She also asked us to luncheons where she had decorated paper bags with a picnic lunch in each bag. As she grew weaker, she would lie on her sofa and smile at us across the room as we sat around the dining room table, partaking of food that she or a helpful friend had made. One day, some months into her illness, she entered a nursing home for special care. Because she lived alone, her friends had tried to do all that they could and a doctor friend Jim had even flown with her to Florida for special treatment of the cancer. But there came a time when nothing was able to help. She spent several weeks there and friends visited her. She was always upbeat and smiling. She cheered us up!

One Sunday after church when I was eating at the college cafeteria in our small town, I was surprised to hear my name paged in the large room. No one had ever been paged there as long as I had been in town. At least I had never heard of such. In other words, it was a highly unusual incident. I went to the office phone in the cafeteria and heard Nancy's voice at the other end of the receiver. She was calling from the nursing home and this is what she said. "Jane, come right away. I am dying this afternoon." It was a crisp order from someone who seemed to know what she was doing. No one ignored Nancy's orders even though they might seem strange.

Hurrying toward Asheville, some seventeen miles away, I walked into Nancy's room and noted that several of her special friends were there and more were coming all the time. They had all been called or paged by her. Nancy looked lovely in her best pink night jacket adorned with lace and pink rosebuds. Her cheeks looked rosy and her yellow gold hair was brushed back from her face. Her make up was flawless.

"Nancy," I said, "what are you up to? You look wonderful. There is no way that you are dying today!" As I spoke, her other friends who were surrounding her bed and sitting on chairs, echoed my sentiments. We all took turns talking and listening to her and passed some time in the usual manner of women who are at a party or gathering. She then said, "I am going to Heaven today. When I am there, I am going to check on that husband of mine who has already been there a long time. I want to see what he has been up to when I haven't been around to keep my eye on him!" She said she would be looking down and checking on us also. I answered that she might not see us as much as she thought since my belief was that Heavenly Beings see only the good in the world and not the bad. We might be found lacking in the area of pure goodness.

About that time the phone rang by her bedside. Her sister-in-law was calling from Florida to check on her. We could hardly believe our ears as we heard her next comment. She answered briskly and firmly in her 'Nancy's way.' "I'm sorry but I have to get off of the phone. I'm dying today and can't talk right now! Call back later!" She acted as matter of fact as if someone called about a hair appointment or a trip to the grocery store.

We, her friends, thought this was very funny and a bit crazy as she looked great and acted like her usual self. Within minutes of this call, she sat up in the bed with a start, obviously in pain. At that precise moment one of her friends, a doctor named Joel, arrived in the room for a visit. He went over to put his arm around her. Suddenly she fell back and color drained from her face. We all watched in a mixture of awe, sorrow and pain at the speed of this transition of the soul leaving the body and parting into Heaven. We observed only an empty shell of the bright spirit that had inhabited this earthly body. Her friend, the doctor, pronounced her dead. She had been correct about her death on that very day. It seemed a great mystery how she was so certain that she knew that this day she was going to her eternal life. She was not now afraid. She had been assured of her future home in that promised place of many mansions.

"I am the resurrection and the life. He who believes on Me, though he may die, he shall live."

—*John 11:25*

As I entered the narthex of the church for the memorial service, I was surprised to see my watercolor of Nancy mounted on an easel just by the entrance to the church auditorium. Right before the service, the minister handed me a paper with two paragraphs about Heaven. The other two and one half pages had been inked out. Our church's two trained theologians had taken a large magic marker and each one had blacked out all my beliefs about Heaven except for two paragraphs. Perhaps my thoughts were correct but too lengthy. I would like to believe that the thoughts had validity. Perhaps there was not time enough in the service to read the three pages. Whatever the correct theology, it didn't matter anymore to Nancy as she now knew the truth about Heaven. We on earth were just guessing!

Heaven

"We've been a glimpse of the real thing, our true home, our resurrection bodies. The Spirit of God whets our appetite by giving us a taste of what's ahead. He puts a little of heaven in our hearts so that we'll never settle for less."

—*2 Corinthians 5:4–5*

This little essay comes about after talking to Nancy about Heaven. She said that she didn't feel at all sure about what they were saying at the churches when they were describing Heaven. These are the words for Nancy I was inspired to write concerning what I believe about Heaven.

"So, God, from what we know of you, you will understand that when we die, we are leaping into the unknown and the thought of it frightens us. We want to see your face. We are eager to see our friends and family who have come to be with you. Will there be an angel there to introduce us to you and put our hands in those of yours? We wonder when The Book of Life will be opened and we wonder what it will say about each of us. We often think about your promises of your going to prepare a place for us. What kind of place is it? You say it will be a mansion with many rooms. In my mind that symbolism could mean that all the people of the earth from the past and present will inhabit all the endless numbers of stars in the Universe. I like to think that all our own ancestors will be together on one star if we want it that way. As for the streets of gold, gold isn't that important to me as seeing my family and old friends but I sort of understand what you are trying to say. The people of the world seem to be thrilled with gold and so the idea of having something wonderful to walk upon probably appeals to them. Gold to many people is a symbol of something good.

Dear Lord, when we hear the Messiah sung or when we experience the gorgeous pinks and purples of the early dawn and twilight, when we feel a deep love in our hearts toward someone or taste certain dishes such as banana pudding, then we know we are seeing only a tiny, tiny evidence of your magnificent Heaven. Just knowing that you have promised to multiply those earthly thrills many times over when we are in Heaven is something that should occupy our minds more often than it does. We have heard that in Heaven there will be no more cruelty, loss of life, illness, angry words, war, and marriage. So then why do we here on earth keep sending "Sympathy" cards when people die? We should send cards of "Congratulations" if we really believe what you have promised to us in your words about Heaven. Most of us have a tendency to be like your disciple Thomas who had to see what was promised with his own eyes in order to believe. We wish you had given us a bit more detail about Heaven but you always know best and I am sure that you had a good reason for just whetting our appetites.

If Heaven is so special as you have promised and if we truly believe your words, then why are we so tongue-tied when we know a family member or friend might die in the next few weeks or months. We want so badly to say something to the one who is going ahead of us, but we do not as it seems to be a forbidden subject. We do have it right when we have a service of celebration in our churches for one who has gone on rather than the old type of funeral where everyone is sobbing and grieving as if that person who has left us behind, will never be seen again.

We have a universal desire to get our closets clean, and our shelves emptied and organized before coming to meet you. Most of our lives we have been busy collecting stuff that is supposed to make us happy. Our homes are full of computers, books, records and clothes. Some of us talk about building a bigger house or a bigger storage room to hold all of these things. We cringe when a minister in the pulpit mentions the verse in the Bible that warns against the building of bigger barns. That verse come too close to home. We pacify ourselves thinking, "Well, God gave certain humans an architectural ability so what is wrong with these great buildings? It would be hiding ones light under a bushel not to use that genius. If these big homes are built, certainly there must be someone out there that needs to buy the bigger houses and barns.

Back to Nancy and others of our friends who say that they *may* go to Heaven before the rest of us. As we all know, your plans often interrupt our plans. We are really looking forward to your explanation of all the questions we have all had for years about your Creation and why you have done the things that you have chosen to do and that you have chosen not to do. We have written books, drawn swords and gotten furious at our own children over many of your mysteries that we don't understand but accept and that they don't understand and often do not accept.

When I come into your presence I want to do what you want me to do, but I also want to see what you had wanted me to do that is written in The Book of Life, I want to see the relatives, family and friends and hear the great music of the angels. I long to be held in your arms as you held the children in Palestine so many years ago and to be told again that you love me. I particularly want to know that you have forgiven me for so many years of making mistakes. I have a lot of hope along that line as I know that you forgave Peter though he denied you, that you forgave David though he took someone else's wife, that you forgave Abraham for pretending that his wife was his sister, and that you forgave hundreds of others for their mistakes in life.

So, God, as you see from this paper which tries to explain what I understand about Heaven, please know that as much as I read your words and the words of great theologians, I still think like a child and speak like a child when I try to tell Nancy and others what Heaven is like. Hopefully, after reading this, she will want to go to Heaven and will know that she will soon be there with you. Amen!

Last Page

o o o o o o o o o o o o o o o o o o o o o o o o o o o o o o o o o o o o o o

"I have fought the good fight. I have finished the race. I have kept the faith."

—2 Timothy 4:7

Here I end this little book which tells of varied experiences in life that have tried my patience, the patience of others and my soul. I would like to say again how grateful I am that God was there to help me endure and overcome whatever happened. In these days of trauma in every part of the world, these personal experiences are small. However, the same simple formula exists in relating to all that is horrific in our lives and in the lives of others. One must pray to the Lord for guidance, pray for His will in helping us deal with the difficulties of life, thank him for all the blessings he has given to us in the midst of the trying times. During those awful times, we should ask for his kind of peace. "Peace I leave with you, my peace I give unto you; not as the world giveth, give I unto you. Let not your heart be troubled, neither let it be afraid." (John 14:27)

We know that others, our friends and neighbors, are also dealing with problems in their lives. In spite of all the theology I have read and theology that I have heard in sermons and classes at seminary, my understanding of God's will and of God's Heaven is simple. "Love your God with all your heart, soul and mind. Lean not to your own understanding but in everything do his will and he will guide your path." (Proverbs 3:5)

In ending this book I would like to borrow the following phrase from my friend Ruth who always jokingly said that she wanted these following words on her tombstone, "End of Construction. Thank you for your patience!"

About the Author

Jane Elizabeth Frist lives in Montreat, North Carolina, a small town just east of Asheville. The town is in the mountains of Western North Carolina and is a conference center and a college town. It is appreciated for its beauty, its lake, hiking trails, and club programs for youth. Quite a few well-known people have lived, worked, studied and been inspired while dwelling in this wonderful place.

Jane's love of writing and drawing began as a young child. She illustrated her mother's book, *No Wings in the Manse*, when she was seventeen.

She had many poems and several stories published in the Agnes Scott College magazine, *The Aurora*. Randall Jarrell, Poet Laureate of the United States in the 50s, awarded second and third places to her in one poetry contest.

She graduated from Agnes Scott College with a BA major in English and a minor in Art. She studied at Princeton Theological Seminary but left to live in Germany while her husband studied at the University of Bonn on a scholarship given by Princeton Seminary and the German government. While in Germany she had the opportunity to spend some time teaching English to the wife of the Korean Ambassador in Germany. She studied German at the University of Heidelberg. After moving to Denver some years later, she received her Master's equivalent at the University of Denver. She taught in the Denver Public Schools between 1968 and 1978. Along with her teaching career she went into Real Estate where she has been for thirty years. In 1993 she began her own company, Frist Realty, as still continues being the Broker/Owner and listing and selling properties throughout the Swannanoa Valley, specializing in Montreat.

In 1997 she wrote the book *Montreat, How I Love You* which was written to celebrate the town's 100th anniversary. She illustrated the book with line drawings. She painted the picture on the cover and added stories and poems about her experiences in Montreat.

This new book, *"Lady, I've Seen Enough!"* Is full of humorous stories she experienced throughout life. There are some line drawings but most of the book contains photographs which illustrate these experiences. The cover is a copy of a painting in watercolor she did of a little house which was inspired by the Montreat Post Office.

978-0-595-41368-3
0-595-41368-4

Printed in the United States
65173LVS00002B/253-348